JOURNEY

TO MATURITY

*Equipping the New Disciple
from a Muslim Background
to Follow Christ*

Journey to Maturity

Equipping the New Disciple from a
Muslim Background to Follow Christ

Copyright © 2019

Global Initiative: Reaching Muslim Peoples

This discipleship plan is the fruition of the doctoral project written by Dr. Ken Ferguson and adapted for book format by the *Global Initiative* Team.

Printed in the United States of America

ISBN: 979-8638183318

Editing and interior layout by Susan Meamber

Cover design by Jennifer Hall

Journey to Maturity

*Equipping Christians to Engage
Muslims with Faith*

TABLE OF CONTENTS

ACKNOWLEDGMENTS

The content of this book comes primarily from the work completed as part of my doctoral project. I want to thank my wife, Kathy, for her patience and support during the research and writing process. I wrote this paper while traveling internationally for the Center for Ministry to Muslims (CMM), now called Global Initiative: Reaching Muslim Peoples (GI). On multiple occasions, I wanted to quit, but she encouraged me to complete the program.

I want to especially acknowledge Dr. Jim Bennett, my project advisor, for his guidance and wise advice through the doctoral process.

In addition, I want to thank Dr. Tommy Hodum and Mel Rogers who made valuable contributions to the content. I am also in debt to my colleagues who reviewed the content and made helpful recommendations, especially Dr. Fred Farrokh, who provided insight as a former Muslim. I appreciate the efforts of

Tommy Hodum who chaired the committee to produce this book. He kept us on assignment.

I would be remiss if I did not mention the director of *Global Initiative*, Mark Brink, who had the vision for this book and provided the support to make it a reality.

And last, but certainly not least, I want to credit Susan Meamber, our office manager, for her editing and layout work. I wish I could have used her as my editor when I originally started my doctoral program in 1998.

I pray that God will use this as a tool to help church leaders and believers fulfill God's command to "go and make disciples of all nations" (Matthew 28:19).

Ken Ferguson

FOREWORD

For several years, I had the privilege of serving as a board member of *Global Initiative: Reaching Muslim Peoples*. I observed their ministry up close and personal and admired their three-fold emphasis. First, *Global Initiative* believes in building a strong network of prayer warriors by promoting the *Jumaa* Prayer Fellowships. Today, more than 60,000 people around the world regularly intercede with *Global Initiative* for the salvation of spiritually lost Muslims.

Second, *Global Initiative* believes its mandate is to equip the church everywhere to reach Muslims with the Good News about Jesus. To date, *Global Initiative* team members have taught more than 50,000 people around world to share the gospel with Muslims. Many new missionaries who serve the Lord in some of the most difficult places on earth received their "call" in a *Global Initiative* equipping venue.

Third, *Global Initiative* recognizes the critical necessity of providing discipleship for new converts from Islam. In the last twenty-five years, more Muslims have become Christians than in all the centuries since Islam's inception in the seventh century!

Spiritual warfare issues for new converts from Islam are uniquely intense and require a distinctively Pentecostal response. The book you are holding, *Journey to Maturity,* draws on decades of Pentecostal field experience. Practitioners who have been there and experienced it—both domestically and internationally—offer their insights and wisdom regarding best practices. Throughout the book, great emphasis is placed on the power and work of the Holy Spirit and the importance of Pentecostal prayer. No suggestion is offered without a powerful and relevant scriptural underpinning.

No doubt many of you have already experienced Muslims in your church or community coming to the Lord. Others have Muslims moving to your area or engage with Muslims in the workplace and you anticipate sharing the gospel with them and discipling them. In either case, you will want copies of *Journey to Maturity* to assist in the discipleship process. I am grateful to *Global Initiative* for producing this book. With more and more Muslims following Jesus as Lord and Savior, it could not have come at a more critical time. It is my honor to highly recommend it to every pastor and worker.

Alton Garrison

Former Assistant Superintendent of the Assemblies of God (U.S.)
and author of *A Spirit Empowered Church*; currently serves
as the Executive Director of the Acts 2 Journey Initiative

DEFINITION OF TERMS

- **Christian**: One who, having repented and received the forgiveness of sins through the sacrificial death and resurrection of Jesus, has submitted to the authority of Jesus Christ in all areas of his or her life and joined the worldwide community called the Church

- **CMB**: A Christian from a Muslim Background

- **Disciple**: An individual who has come to a saving knowledge of Jesus and had chosen to follow Him, has renounced Islam, and has become a part of the worldwide Christian community

- **Disciple-maker**: A person who, through prayer and cooperation with the Holy Spirit, is striving to see Muslims come to a saving knowledge of Jesus, be baptized, welcomed into the community of believers, and go on to maturity in Christ through discipleship.

- **Imminent**: Refers to God's presence and nearness to mankind

- **Maturity**: The outcome of Christ being formed in you (Galatians 4:19; Ephesians 4:13; Philippians 3:12-14)

- **Paraclete**: This term comes from the Greek word *paracletos*, which refers to one who is called alongside of. This "Helper" was further identified as the Spirit of Truth in John 14:17; Jesus clearly identified the Paraclete as the Holy Spirit (verse 26). Various translations refer to the Paraclete as the Comforter, Counselor, or Advocate.

- **Pentecostal**: A Christian who emphasizes the experience of the gifts of the Holy Spirit as displayed in the book of Acts, with particular attention to speaking in tongues as the initial physical evidence of being filled with the Holy Spirit. The Pentecostal Christian believes that these gifts of the Spirit are for today and are imperative for emboldening the witness and for edifying the Church.

- **Sacrament**: a religious ceremony or ritual in the Christian Church, such as water baptism or Holy Communion

- **Transcendence**: God's separation from and exaltation above creation

REJOICE! THE KINGDOM OF
GOD IS GROWING!

"Can you tell me why Christ had to die?" asked Yusuf sincerely. The question came as a shock to the Christian disciple-maker, who had just met this elderly Muslim man. It was evident that the Holy Spirit was working in Yusuf's heart. Over the course of the next several moments, the disciple-maker shared the story of the gospel with this man. He related how Jesus came to die for his sins to satisfy God's justice, and how no amount of good works could cancel all the wrongs he had done. With wide eyes, Yusuf exclaimed, "No one has ever explained these things to me before!" When asked if he wanted to make Jesus the Lord of his life, he simply replied, "Sure, why not?"

Over the last several decades, millions of Muslims have given their lives to Christ. The Kingdom of God is advancing in the Muslim world, a reality that is cause for rejoicing! All over the world, people like Yusuf have said "yes" to Jesus. Although it seems that his conversion was quick and dramatic, there is no telling how many other Christians planted seeds in his heart prior to this conversation. Indeed, for many Muslims throughout the world, coming to a saving knowledge of Christ is a journey.

The time a disciple-maker invests in leading someone to Christ may pale in comparison to the days and months one should devote to discipling a new believer from a Muslim background. Paul's words from 1 Thessalonians 2:8 are poignant: *"We were ready to share with you not only the gospel of God but also our own selves, because you had become very dear to us."*

We, at *Global Initiative: Reaching Muslim Peoples*, pray that this resource will be a blessing for you, whether you are a disciple-maker who is discipling a new believer from a Muslim background or a new disciple. Over the past forty years, the Church has seen a 2,000% increase in the number of Christians from a Muslim Background (CMBs).[1] May the worldwide Church be faithful to both share the gospel and disciple the people the Holy Spirit brings into His Kingdom, leading them on a journey to maturity in Christ.

---

[1] Patrick Johnstone and Duane Miller, "Believers in Christ from a Muslim Background: A Global Census," *Interdisciplinary Journal of Research on Religion* 11 (2015): 11.

# HOW TO USE THIS BOOK

This book, divided into two parts, is designed for both the disciple-maker and the new disciple. The first part provides a brief overview of some important beliefs and practices of Islam. Because of our desire for this resource to be used around the globe and because Islam is not monolithic, this overview is presented in broad strokes. Following each Islamic belief statement, we provide a statement of biblical truth to counter the previously cited Islamic claims. Please read these aloud and continue by praying the attached prayer. This overview will prove beneficial in the discipleship of CMBs, especially if the disciple-maker has limited knowledge of Islam. The disciple will also find this helpful, particularly as he or she learns to compare and contrast Islamic teachings with Christian theological truths.

In Part Two, Your Pentecostal Journey to Maturity, one finds ten lessons designed to lead the new believer to maturity in Christ. This part can be used in two different ways. A disciple-maker could go through these ten lessons with a CMB or group of CMBs. Because of the format, it would be ideal for both the disciple-maker and the CMB to have his or her own copy of Part Two. Access to a Bible is also a necessity.

In some instances, a disciple-maker may not be available to help the CMB. Perhaps the new believer learned about Christ on the television or Internet. In such circumstances, the new believer could use this as a self-study. Here, CMBs will be encouraged as they walk through these ten lessons, knowing that they are never alone. Indeed, God has promised that He will never leave them or forsake them (Hebrews 13:5). Therefore, the CMB, with Bible and pen in hand, can engage in the discipleship process using the discipleship guide in Part Two.

This resource is not to be used as a permanent substitute for community. We pray that new believers will seek out and be welcomed into a church family. The Lord is finding lost sheep among the people of Islam; may all whom He finds be invited into discipleship!

Part 1

Understanding Islamic Beliefs and Practices

THE IMPERATIVE OF
DISCIPLESHIP

It's been 2,000 years since the birth of the Church and many books on discipleship have been written. You might be thinking, "So, is another book on becoming a follower of Christ necessary?" It all depends on the intended audience. Yes, ample materials are available for the "Westerner" or individual from a Judeo-Christian background. Much has been written to inform, suggest, and guide the disciple-maker in leading disciples from this context. However, a dearth exists that focuses on Christians from a Muslim Background (CMB). In a recent survey conducted by *Global Initiative*, people made some notable comments:

"You asked if we would use CMB discipleship materials. Are you kidding, of course!" *Missionary/Pastor*

"One of the leaders in a large Pentecostal church called her aside and said, "Noor, we have a large number of CMBs coming into the church. We don't have any discipleship materials to give them. Can you help us?"

"*Yes to a new resource*! Most of what we have has been developed by non-AG and/or non-Pentecostal folks. I know our folks want quality resources to help in discipleship. It's very needed." *Missionary*

We need discipleship material that deals with the baptism in the Holy Spirit and the rejection of Islam as a faith! *Missionary*

"If *Global Initiative: Reaching Muslim Peoples* created new material for discipling new Christians from a Muslim background I would 100% use it!" *A national church leader of the most populous Islamic country in the world*

Spiritual formation of new believers presents a challenge in the best of circumstances. When one considers the vast differences between Muslims and Christians, the challenge becomes apparent. If the disciple lives in an Islamic society, the challenge increases exponentially. Islamic society seeks to isolate converts to Christianity from society, silence their witness, and pressure them to revert to Islam. Don McCurry summarizes this perspective: "It should be remembered that when Orthodox Muslims discuss the idea of 'religious freedom,' they mean that all others are free to become Muslims, but Muslims are not free to change their religion."[2]

Don McCurry goes on to relate the realities that Christians can experience while living in Muslim countries. The list includes going to jail for leading Muslims to Jesus, emigrating to avoid imprisonment, seeing expatriates deported, experiencing church burnings and murders, having prayer meetings for expatriates closed, Bibles confiscated, and watching as cruel economic pressure is placed upon impoverished Christians to get them to convert to Islam. If it is difficult for Christian disciple-makers to operate in Islamic society, how complex is it for Christians from a Muslim Background to live normal lives, function in society, or

---

[2] Don McCurry, *Healing the Broken Family of Abraham: New Life for Muslims* (Colorado Springs, CO: Ministries to Muslims, 2011), 294.

mature as new believers in the church? Martyrdom is not uncommon among Muslim converts.

The various accounts of the Great Commission provide the blueprint for missions: evangelism, discipleship, church planting, and leadership training. If the church neglects any of these components, it will fail. Fulfilling the Great Commission includes going, baptizing, and teaching, but the goal of the Great Commission is to make disciples. Jesus placed the responsibility of discipleship upon His disciples. Similarly, He obliged new believers to be baptized and to observe all of His commands. Thus, Jesus defines discipleship as identification with the Father, Son, and Holy Spirit and as obedience to His teaching. Jesus commissioned the Church to make disciples out of all nations.

Further, Jesus repeatedly asked His disciples to follow Him. Three of the four Gospel accounts record the admonition *"If anyone wishes to come after Me, he must deny himself, and take up his cross and follow Me"* (Matthew 16:24; Mark 8:34; Luke 9:23).[3] Following Jesus includes journeying through life with Him. However, Islam has depicted Jesus as someone other than Immanuel (God with us) and makes the recognition of the biblical Christ impossible. Failure to acknowledge or understand Christ for who He is and what He has done makes following Him extremely difficult. This fact has continually hindered the disciple-makers' ability to assist followers in becoming true disciples.

Minimal success in church planting among Islamic societies underscores the church's inability to produce a significant number of healthy disciples from a Muslim background. Under the best of circumstances, Christians struggle to live in Islamic societies. Persecution, restrictions on the church, anti-conversion laws, and government support for Islam all create hardships for churches. Some Islamic societies have zero tolerance for any religion other than Islam. They forbid prayer meetings and even the possession of Bibles. In such cases, churches often neglect evangelism and

---

[3] All scriptural quotations, unless otherwise noted, are from the English Standard Version and are italicized.

discipleship. Christians struggle to merely survive. Life is even more difficult for Christians from a Muslim Background (CMBs). Family and society put incredible pressure upon these converts to revert to Islam. A number of them withstand the pressure, but some succumb and return to the mosque. Others emigrate for survival, thus eliminating the potential for witness in their communities. Although extraction provides physical safety and security to practice their faith, it does nothing to build churches in Islamic societies.

All of these factors necessitated the writing of this Pentecostal discipleship material that considers the distinct worldview, theological perspective, and cultural value system of Muslims. Too many CMBs have reverted to Islam. The successful spiritual formation of converts from Islam requires recognizing the problems with Islamic beliefs and practices and the acceptance of Christian beliefs, values, and practices. Disciple-makers must teach the Bible in such a way that clearly distinguishes sound biblical doctrine from ideologies and cultural practices in Islamic societies that are detrimental to true discipleship. Furthermore, disciple-makers must distinguish biblical truth from church culture that is not biblical, whether the practices represent the host national church or the sending church of a particular missionary. This might include, but is not limited to, issues such as church government, music, dress, and gender roles.

The disciple-maker who is unfamiliar with Islam will encounter a religion that appears to be similar to Christianity but, in fact, contradicts the most basic tenets of biblical Christian faith. Islam teaches an attractive form of monotheism and salvation by works. However, the disciple-maker will unmask a religious system that attempts to diminish the person and work of Jesus Christ, deemphasize the relational nature of God, and trivialize the sinful nature of humankind.

Disciples in Islamic societies often struggle to grow spiritually. It is imperative that discipleship programs help build strong Christians who not only stand under the fire of persecution, but share their faith effectively in an oppressive environment. *Our goal is to assist Muslim converts in making the transition from an*

Islamic community to a Christian community by helping them grow in Christ and understand Christian beliefs and practices. Pentecostal discipleship teaches the nature of spiritual warfare. This material will teach and encourage the CMB to resist Satan, pray in the Spirit, and seek the enablement of the Holy Spirit for effective ministry.

Both Islam and Christianity are monotheistic religions, but history shows that Christianity's most cherished articles of faith—such as the sinfulness of humankind, the Trinity, the sonship and deity of Christ, the death, resurrection, and glorification of Jesus—are anathema to Muslims. Even though a CMB may express sufficient faith for salvation, his or her discipleship entails the monumental task of transitioning from one end of the theological and cultural spectrum to the other. A discipleship process that does not take into account these vast differences will neither establish mature believers nor assist in the process of planting indigenous churches in Islamic societies.

In recent history, attention has not been directed at these discrepancies but on a *middle of the road approach.* Over the past few decades, many people in ministry to Muslims have focused on hypothetical concepts, bridge building, dynamic equivalence, and the supposed similarities between the religions. This has ultimately created confusion in evangelism and problems with discipleship. It has even led some to teach the prophethood of Muhammad and the erroneous belief that the Quran contains true revelation. This is extremely problematic because the clarity and simplicity of the gospel has been lost in endeavoring to appease Muslims with a message that does not intentionally contradict their Islamic beliefs.

In order to claim truth, one must always look at the whole, not a part or just a piece. Consider these questions: Can or has Islam saved anyone? Is there another means of salvation outside of the substitutionary death of Jesus Christ? The answers to these questions determine the acceptance and understanding needed as we examine the great differences in Islamic belief and Christian belief. Muslims and some Christians advocate the idea that both monotheistic faiths believe in and pray to the same God. However, the facts reveal that we have very different views. Therefore, throughout this book, we will refer to the Muslim god as Allah

THEOLOGICAL DIFFERENCES BETWEEN CHRISTIANITY AND ISLAM

Christians from a Muslim Background have obviously assented to sufficient truth concerning Jesus Christ for salvation, but most carry heavy theological baggage. While beliefs differ somewhat among Muslims, they all share common expressions of faith.

Differing Beliefs Regarding Sin

Islamic Perspective of Sin

Sin's impact on a person's relationship with God poses one of the chief theological distinctions between Islam and Christianity. The Quran provides an account of Adam's sin and its consequences: "Then did Satan make them slip from the (Garden), and get them out of the state (of felicity) in which they had been. We said: 'Get ye down, all (ye people), with enmity between yourselves. On earth will be your dwelling place and your means of livelihood—for a time'" (Quran 2:36).[4] Furthermore, the Quran seems to teach that sin has negatively affected the human race: "Nor do I absolve my own self (of blame): the (human) soul is certainly prone to evil, unless my Lord do bestow His Mercy" (Quran 12:53). John Gilchrist, however, makes the following observation:

> Muslim scholars have always taught that sins are no more than acts of wrongdoing, breaches of the laws of Islam, which can be remedied by good deeds, repentance and the forgiveness of Allah. Sinfulness, as a state of the soul motivating mankind instinctively towards evil, does not come into the Islamic equation.[5]

Since Muslims do not believe in original sin, they believe that people neither possess a sinful nature nor inherit the guilt of Adam's sin. The Quran speaks more about acts of sin than sinful nature—people committing sins against themselves not against Allah. Sins damage the life and status of the sinner, but they cannot affect Allah's absolute greatness as Quran 2:54 illustrates: "And remember Moses said to his people: 'O my people! Ye have indeed wronged yourselves by your worship of the calf.'"

Muslims believe that people make mistakes because of their weaknesses, thus needing guidance instead of changed natures. "Allah doth wish to lighten your (difficulties): For man was created weak (in flesh)" (Quran 4:28). Muslims not only oppose the Christian view of original sin, but they also believe in the basic goodness of people. Muslims believe that all children are born into the Islamic faith. Badru D. Kateregga and David Shenk explain the Muslim position:

---

[4] All Qur'anic quotations, unless otherwise noted, are from Abdullah Yusuf Ali, *The Meaning of the Holy Quran: New Edition with Revised Translation, Commentary, and Newly Compiled Comprehensive Index,* 10th ed. (Beltsville, MD: Amana Publications, 2001).

[5] John Gilchrist, *Sharing the Gospel with Muslims* (Cape Town, South Africa: Life Challenge, 2003), 23.

As Muslims we do not accuse Adam and Eve of transmitting sin and evil to the whole of mankind. The two were absolved of their sin, and their descendants were made immune from its effect. Sin is not original, hereditary, or inevitable. It is not from Allah. It is acquirable through choice, but also avoidable through knowledge and true guidance from Allah. Muslims believe that man is fundamentally a good and dignified creature. He is not a fallen being.[6]

Consequently, Muslims do not sense their need for redemption or regeneration. They believe that no one can bear the sins of another; every individual must account for his or her own actions.

Biblical Truth Regarding Sin

For the wrath of God is revealed from heaven against all ungodliness and unrighteousness of men, who by their unrighteousness suppress the truth. (Romans 1:18)

For all have sinned and fall short of the glory of God. (Romans 3:23)

Sin is more than a mistake or "slip." Wrong belief of what sin is creates wrong belief regarding salvation. William Evans presents a solid understanding of the biblical teaching regarding sin:

If sin is regarded as merely an offence against man, a weakness of human nature, a mere disease, rather than as rebellion, transgression, and enmity against God, and therefore something condemning and punishable, we shall not, of course see any necessity for the atonement. We must see sin as the Bible depicts it—as something which brings wrath, condemnation, and eternal ruin in its train.[7]

---

[6] Badru D. Kateregga and David Shenk, *Islam and Christianity: A Muslim and a Christian in Dialogue* (Ibadan, Nigeria: Daystar Press, 1980), 107-108.

[7] William Evans, *The Great Doctrines of the Bible*, rev. ed. (Grand Rapids, MI: Moody Press, 1949), 78.

Prayer

Lord Jesus, as a Disciple-maker and Disciple, help me to see and believe the biblical record of what sin is and what it has done to mankind. I rebuke and bind any and all deception that would cause me or another person to believe anything that would distort or corrupt the truth. AMEN!

Differing Beliefs Regarding God

Islamic Perspective Regarding Allah

The concept of Allah appears complex in Islamic theology. Muslims believe in the oneness of Allah and in his absolute sovereignty. Allah has no partners; he exists independent of creation. He revealed his will and law through the archangel Gabriel. Muslims affirm the unity of Allah (*tawhid*) as a fundamental Islamic concept. The first line of the Muslim's confession of faith (*shahada*) explains clearly the dual concept of *tawhid*: "There is no god except Allah." That statement means that no god exists except Allah, and no god exists like Allah. It implies oneness in number and uniqueness in quality. Muhammad taught that Allah has no companions or equals (Quran 112:1-4). Muslims consider anthropomorphisms (giving a human trait to a non-human entity) inappropriate when referring to Allah. *Shirk*, the most grievous of all sins, means the association of partners or equals with Allah. A person cannot reach, comprehend, or influence Allah in any way. Although Allah transcends his creation and remains totally separate from it, the Quran pictures Allah closer than a person's own jugular (Quran 50:16). *Sufi* Muslims use this verse to support their idea of intimacy with Allah, but orthodox Muslims abhor the idea. As creator, Allah knows people better than they know themselves.

Christians, when discussing the attributes of God, usually mention love and holiness. Although Muslims agree with the concept of the holiness of Allah, they do not speak much about his love. Allah's love means approval of creation, not intimacy with creation. As humanity's watchful lord, Allah demands obedience.

Their concept of revelation is one of transcendence. Allah reveals his will but not his nature.

Muslims prefer to talk about Allah's power and sovereignty. They repeat the statement, *"Allahu akbar"* (Allah is great), many times every day. This practice, known as *takbir*, means "to declare greatness."[8] *Allahu akbar* literally means, "Allah is greater than all" and can be translated as "Allah is most great."[9] Allah directs his creation according to his sovereignty, thus filling the hearts of Muslims with fear. As "Lord of the Worlds" (Quran 1:2),[10] Allah will direct what he has created. *Tawhid* and *takbir* best describe the Muslim's concept of deity. Islam, the name of the religion, means submission; Allah reveals his will, and all of creation must submit. Islam teaches that people need guidance to submit and follow the right path, or they will take the path to judgment.

Later in the book we will address issues concerning the nature of God, such as immanence and transcendence, emphasizing God's personal attributes such as love, goodness, and benevolence. Muslims focus on transcendence, but they do not believe in immanence. Likewise, they tend to emphasize the omnipotence and sovereignty of Allah. They believe that if Allah had any personal or moral attributes it would limit him.

Since the Muslim understanding of the oneness of Allah excludes the possibility of the deity of Jesus or the Holy Spirit (Quran 5:73), we must emphasize the uniqueness of Jesus Christ. Assuming that the disciple has already assented to the truth of Jesus Christ as the Son of God and God's sacrifice for the sins of the world, this book will fortify the new believer's comprehension of the Christian concept of the Godhead.

---

[8] Cyril Glasse, *The Concise Encyclopedia of Islam*, ed. J. Peter Hobson (San Francisco, CA: Harper and Row, 1989), 394.

[9] Glasse, *The Concise Encyclopedia of Islam*, 24.

[10] Mohammad Marmaduke Pickthall, *The Meaning of the Glorious Koran: An Explanatory Translation*, trans. Mohammad Marmaduke Pickthall (New York, NY: New American Library, 1953).

Biblical Truth Regarding God

Hear, O Israel: The LORD our God, the LORD is one. (Deuteronomy 6:4)

You are my witnesses," declares the LORD,
and my servant whom I have chosen,
that you may know and believe me
and understand that I am he.
Before me no god was formed,
nor shall there be any after me.
I, I am the LORD,
and besides me there is no savior. (Isaiah 43:10-11)

Go therefore and make disciples of all nations, baptizing them in the name of the Father and of the Son and of the Holy Spirit, teaching them to observe all that I have commanded you. And behold, I am with you always, to the end of the age. (Matthew 28:19-20)

And the Holy Spirit descended on him in bodily form, like a dove; and a voice came from heaven, "You are my beloved Son; with you I am well pleased." (Luke 3:22)

The one true God has revealed himself as the eternally self-existent "I am," the Creator of heaven and earth, and the Redeemer of mankind. He has further revealed himself as embodying the principles of relationship and association as Father, Son, and Holy Spirit.[11]

Prayer

Dear God, as a Disciple-maker and Disciple, help me to see and believe the biblical record of who You really are, as Father, Son, and Holy Spirit. With faith from You, I will believe what You have done and what You want to accomplish in me. I renounce any and all misinformation. AMEN!

---

[11] P. C. Nelson, *Bible Doctrines* (Springfield, MO: Gospel Publishing House, 2009), 19.

Differing Beliefs Regarding Jesus Christ

Islamic Perspective Regarding Jesus Christ

Although Muhammad denied the deity of Jesus, he held a high view of Jesus as a prophet. According to Muhammad, Allah sent Jesus as a messenger to the people of Israel (Quran 5:75). The Quran speaks more highly of Jesus than any other prophet. The Quran even affirms the virgin birth of Jesus. He had no human father, but Allah breathed into the womb of the Virgin Mary (Quran 66:12).

According to the Quran, the Holy Spirit strengthened Jesus (Quran 2:253), and it refers to Jesus as a "Spirit proceeding from Him [Allah]" (Quran 4:171). Furthermore, the Quran names Jesus as "Christ" and says that He will be "held in honour in this world and in the Hereafter and of (the company of) those nearest to Allah" (Quran 3:45). Moreover, Muslims oppose the Christian belief that Jesus is the Son of God. Muhammad seems to have misunderstood the Christian belief in the Trinity as the Father, the Mother, and the Son (Quran 5:116). They understand Christians to mean that God fathered a child by natural means with Mary: "Say: He is Allah, the One and Only; Allah, the Eternal, Absolute; He begetteth not nor is He begotten; and there is none like unto Him" (Quran 112:1-4). The idea that Allah had a son in this manner offends Muslims: "It is not befitting to (the majesty of) Allah that He should beget a son. Glory be to Him" (Quran 19:35)! "Indeed ye have put forth a thing most monstrous" (Quran 19:89)! In his commentary on this verse, Yusuf Ali briefly explains the Islamic position on the belief that Jesus is the Son of God and the belief concerning His substitutionary atonement:

The belief in Allah begetting a son is not a question of words or of speculative thought. Muslims believe it is a stupendous blasphemy against Allah and would lower Allah to the level of an animal. If combined with the doctrine of vicarious atonement, it amounts to a negation of Allah's justice and man's personal responsibility. In Islam, the incarnation is believed to be destructive of all moral and spiritual order, and is condemned in the strongest possible terms.[12]

Early Muslims collected oral traditions, wrote them down, and classified them. These stories, known as *Hadith*, record the sayings and deeds of Muhammad. *Hadith* means, "that which is spoken." *Hadith* show how Muhammad interpreted the Quran. There are six major collections of Sunni *Hadith*, and Muslims regard Al-Bukhari's collection, compiled about 200 years after Muhammad's death, as the most reliable, but he says little about Jesus. However, some collections of *Hadith* do address the sin of *shirk*, which is the association of anyone or anything with Allah. *Shirk* is the most severe kind of blasphemy and the most serious sin: "Narrated by Abu Huraira: The Prophet said, 'Whoever dies while still worshipping anything other than Allah as a rival to Allah, will enter Hell (Fire)'" (Hadith 6:24).[13] Knowing that Christians ascribe deity to Jesus, Muslims make every effort to avoid blasphemy, and they consider Christians to be polytheists.

Biblical Truth Regarding Jesus Christ

"She will bear a son, and you shall call his name Jesus, for he will save his people from their sins." All this took place to fulfill what the Lord had spoken by the prophet: "Behold, the virgin shall conceive and bear a son, and they shall call his name Immanuel" (which means, God with us). (Matthew 1:21-23)

Now when Jesus came into the district of Caesarea Philippi, he asked his disciples, "Who do people say that the Son of Man is?" And they said, "Some say John the Baptist, others say Elijah, and others Jeremiah or one of the prophets." He said to them, "But who do you say that I am?" Simon Peter replied, "You are the Christ, the Son of the living God." And Jesus answered him, "Blessed are you, Simon Bar-Jonah! For flesh

---

[12] Ali, *The Meaning of the Holy Quran*, 762.

[13] Sahih Al-Bukhari. *Hadith*, trans. Islamic University Al-Medina Al-Munawwara (Beirut, Lebanon: Dar Al Arabia, 1980), Hadith 6:24.

and blood has not revealed this to you, but my Father who is in heaven. (Matthew 16:13-17)

Zenas J. Bicket succinctly describes the biblical understanding of who Jesus is: "The supernatural birth of Jesus, His sinless life, His working of miracles all give proof that He is the divine Son of God who came to earth in human form to give himself as the ultimate sacrifice for our sins."[14]

Prayer

Lord Jesus, as a Disciple-maker and Disciple, I have asked myself the question, "Who are you?" By the work of your Spirit that leads and guides into all truth, help me to see, accept, and fully believe that You are the Son of God who died for my sins. I renounce any non-biblical teaching that minimizes your birth, life, death, resurrection, and return. Truly, be my Savior and Lord for "You are the Christ, the Son of the living God." (Matthew 16:16)

Differing Beliefs Regarding the Holy Spirit

Islamic Perspective Regarding the Holy Spirit

Muslims believe Allah only communicated a little information about the Holy Spirit to Muhammad (Quran 17:85). The Holy Spirit from Allah strengthened Christ (Quran 2:87) and brought down the Quran (Quran 16:102). Yusuf Ali identifies the Holy Spirit as the title for Gabriel through whom the revelation came down.[15]

According to Luke and John, Jesus told His disciples that after He had ascended, God would send the Holy Spirit (Luke 24:49; John 14:16; Acts 1:8). In John 14:26, Jesus clearly identified the Paraclete as the Holy Spirit. The Quran also refers to one coming after Jesus, "Whose name shall be Ahmad" (Quran 61:6). Muslim scholars understand this as a prediction of the coming of

---

[14] Zenas J. Bicket, "Our 16 Doctrines," Brochure (Springfield, MO: Gospel Publishing House, 2017), 5.

[15] Ali, *The Meaning of the Holy Quran*, 664.

Muhammad. Some even say that Muhammad actually claimed to be the Paraclete of John 14:16.

Biblical Truth Regarding the Holy Spirit

John 14:16-17 declares, *"And I will ask the Father, and he will give you another Helper, to be with you forever, even the Spirit of truth, whom the world cannot receive, because it neither sees him nor knows him. You know him, for he dwells with you and will be in you."* This verse speaks of the Holy Spirit, the third person of the Trinity, who convicts the world of sin (John 16:8) and guides believers in the Truth (John 16:13). This same Holy Spirit filled the believers on the Day of Pentecost, empowering them to be witnesses (Acts 1:8). This miraculous indwelling, referred to as the baptism in the Holy Spirit, was evidenced by speaking in tongues (Acts 2:4; 10:44-47; 19:6) and is available to every believer today (Acts 2:39; see also Part Two, Lesson Seven).

Prayer

Lord Jesus, I recognize it is your Spirit that has brought me to acknowledge my need for You to do for me what I could not do for myself. I also believe You are present to teach me and help me remember Your work and words. I fully reject all the lies and misinformation about someone else being "the comforter" and all non-biblical teaching regarding the Holy Spirit. I will and do believe the biblical account. Lord Jesus, I want to be filled with the Holy Spirit in the same manner as described in these biblical passages.

Differing Beliefs Regarding Angels

Islamic Perspective Regarding Angels

Muslims believe in angels. They believe that Allah created angels from light and endowed them with life, reason, and speech. Angels do not need to eat or drink, and they do not procreate. They praise and glorify Allah and serve as Allah's messengers (Quran 35:1). The Quran mentions some of the archangels by name. The most notable archangel, Gabriel (*Jibril*), brought down all of Allah's messages to the prophets and announced the coming birth of Christ to Mary. Angels introduced the concept of intercession into Islam because they seek forgiveness for believers (Quran 40:7; 53:26). Collections of *Hadith* give most of the details concerning the work of angels. Some angels record the good and bad deeds of Muslims, while others interrogate the dead in their graves. Some oversee the scrolls, while still others oversee Paradise and Hell.

Guardian angels, evil angels, and the lesser spirits (*jinn*), all interact with humans. Good *jinn* give minor help to Muslims while evil *jinn* cause minor irritations. Belief in *jinn* existed in pre-Islamic Arabia and carried over into Islam. Satan rebelled against Allah (Quran 2:34), and he leads all demonic forces.

While all Muslims believe in angels, they disagree considerably as to the extent that angels intrude into their lives. Modern Muslims do not want to be perceived as naive enough to believe in the unseen world. However, millions of ordinary Muslims believe that the spirit world interacts with them daily.

Biblical Truth Regarding Angels

Yes, a spiritual world exists beyond our human perception. Scripture provides the following admonition:

Let no one deceive you with empty words, for because of these things the wrath of God comes upon the sons of disobedience. Therefore, do not become partners with them; for at one time you were darkness, but now you are light in the Lord. Walk as children of light (for the fruit of light is found in all that is good and right and true), and try to discern what is pleasing to the Lord. Take no part in the unfruitful works of darkness, but instead expose them. For it is shameful even to speak of the things that they do in secret. But when anything is exposed by the light, it becomes visible. (Ephesians 5:6-13)

Submit yourselves therefore to God. Resist the devil, and he will flee from you. (James 4:7)

Prayer

Lord Jesus, help me! I want to and need to trust You. I want to and need to believe Your Word. I reject the superstitious beliefs of my past and again ask You to be Lord over my life, my thoughts, and my memories.

Differing Beliefs Regarding Prophets

Islamic Perspective Regarding Prophets

Belief in the prophets is, as the confession of faith (*shahada*) shows, second in importance only to belief in the unity of Allah in the Quran. Muslims believe that Allah sent a prophet to people of every age with the same message (Quran 2:136). The Quran identifies twenty-five prophets. Tradition puts the number of the prophets at 124,000.

Islamic prophets usually include three characteristics. First, Allah endowed each one with a special quality of inspiration called *wahy*. Second, they kept themselves pure. The Quran portrayed all of the prophets as human and, except for Jesus, as in need of Allah's forgiveness. Later, Islamic theology evolved such that all of the prophets were viewed as sinless. Third, prophets possessed the ability to perform miracles. Muhammad never claimed to perform miracles; he only claimed to warn people (Quran 29:50). Muslims believe the miracle of producing the Quran testified to his vocation. The Hadith attributes many miracles to the Prophet. Orthodox Muslims have always considered Muhammad as the final prophet of Allah.

Biblical Truth Regarding Prophets

If a prophet or a dreamer of dreams arises among you and gives you a sign or a wonder, and the sign or wonder that he tells you comes to pass, and if he says, "Let us go after other gods," which you have not known, "and let us serve them," you shall not listen to the words of that prophet or that dreamer of dreams. For the LORD your God is testing you, to know whether you love the LORD your God with all your heart and with all your soul. You shall walk after the LORD your God and fear him and keep his commandments and obey his voice, and you shall serve him and hold fast to him. (Deuteronomy 13:1-4)

When you come into the land that the LORD your God is giving you, you shall not learn to follow the abominable practices of those nations. ... "The LORD your God will raise up for you a prophet like me <u>from among you, from your brothers</u>—it is to him you shall listen. ... I will raise up for them a prophet like you <u>from among their brothers</u>. And I will put my words in his mouth, and he shall speak to them all that I command him. And whoever will not listen to my words that he shall speak in my name, I myself will require it of him. But the prophet who presumes to speak a word in my name that I have not commanded him to speak, or who speaks in the name of other gods, that same prophet shall die.' And if you say in your heart, 'How may we know the word that the LORD has not spoken?'—when a prophet speaks in the name of the LORD, if the word does not come to pass or come true, that is a word that the LORD has not spoken; the prophet has spoken it presumptuously. You need not be afraid of him. (Deuteronomy 18:9, 15, 18-22)

Prayer

Lord Jesus, I pray and believe Your Word! 1 Peter 2:21 warns me: "But false prophets also arose among the people, just as there will be false teachers among you, who will secretly bring in destructive heresies, even denying the Master who bought them, bringing upon themselves swift destruction." And 1 John 4:1 declares, "Beloved, do not believe every spirit, but test the spirits to see whether they are from God, for many false prophets have gone out into the world." I renounce falsehood in all areas of my life. I rebuke the author and influencer of deception in Jesus' name.

Differing Beliefs Regarding the Scriptures

Islamic Perspective Regarding the Scriptures

Muslims believe that Allah sent down (*tanzil*) sacred Scriptures to the prophets. For instance, the Quran is the exact copy of the original in heaven. Muslims agree that the previous books have been lost, and only the final four remain: the Torah (*tawrat*) given to Moses, the Psalms (*zabur*) given to David, the Gospel (*injil*) given to Jesus, and the Quran given to Muhammad.

If Allah sent down all of the books, how do Muslims reconcile differences between the teachings in the Quran and the Bible? Some suggest that the Jews and Christians corrupted the texts. They claim that Christians altered the text to show Jesus as the Son of God. Allah gave the previous books, locked in time and culturally specific for Jews and Christians, but the Quran was for all people of all time. Muslims believe the Quran corrects mistakes in the previous revelations and that it is the final revelation: "By Allah, We (also) sent (Our prophets) to peoples before thee: … And We sent down the Book to thee for the express purpose, that thou shouldst make clear to them those things in which they differ, and that it should be a guide and a mercy to those who believe" (Quran 16:63-64).

Some Muslims do not agree that Allah would allow holy books to be falsified. Most have not read the books and do not know what the Old Testament and New Testament teach. Furthermore, most Muslims consider the question of the previous scriptures as irrelevant. They believe in all of the sacred books and that the Quran affirms them, but they believe that they only need the Quran for guidance.

The prayer in the first *sura* of the Quran contains a petition for guidance: "Show us the straight way, the way of those on whom Thou hast bestowed Thy Grace, those whose (portion) is not wrath, and who go not astray" (Quran. 1:6-7). The god of Islam guides his people by revelation: "Thus doth Allah make His signs clear unto you: that ye may be guided" (Quran 3:103). The Quran does not reveal Allah to Muslims; it reveals Allah's will and law, i.e., guidance. The Islamic view concerning revelation and guidance matches the Islamic concept of sin. People do not inherit guilt. Muslims believe they need neither a redeemer nor a savior; they need guidance to keep them from sinning.

Muslims believe that Allah revealed his law and his will to Muhammad by sending it down through the angel Gabriel (*Jibril*) (Quran 2:97; 16:64). As Muhammad received revelation, he recited it, and others recorded what Muhammad recited. Thus, Muslims believe that their Quran is the exact copy of Allah's book in heaven. Christians believe that God revealed himself and His plan of salvation in the Bible as He inspired prophets and apostles and others to write by the Holy Spirit. Choosing not to use individuals as typewriters, the Holy Spirit moved upon them using each one's personality, education, and experience to produce the exact message God wanted.

Biblical Truth Regarding the Scriptures

"We believe that (1) the Scriptures are God's Word and way of revealing himself to humankind, (2) they are infallible (never wrong), and (3) they are the divinely authoritative guide for our faith, belief and way of living."[16]

And how from childhood you have been acquainted with the sacred writings, which are able to make you wise for salvation through faith in Christ Jesus. All Scripture is breathed out by God and profitable for teaching, for reproof, for correction, and for training in righteousness, that the man of God may be complete, equipped for every good work. (2 Timothy 3:15-17)

For no prophecy was ever produced by the will of man, but men spoke from God as they were carried along by the Holy Spirit." (1 Peter 1:21)

Prayer

Lord Jesus, I need the Holy Spirit to make the Scriptures the foundation of my faith. I want to remember them, share them, and live them out in my walk with You. Please help me as I study them to place myself under Your care as You conform me into Your image.

---

[16] Bicket, "Our 16 Doctrines," 4.

Differing Beliefs Regarding Salvation

Islamic Perspectives Regarding Salvation

While various sects and schisms of Islam believe differently about salvation, Sunni Muslims (the largest group) perceive salvation as overcoming the effects of sins: "But Allah will deliver the righteous to their place of salvation: no evil shall touch them, nor shall they grieve" (Quran 39:61). Muslims believe that reciting the confession of faith makes it possible to enter Paradise, but most believe that they will have to spend some time in the fires of purgatory before admission. Many Muslims believe that Allah, in his sovereignty, decrees salvation or damnation. Some trust Muhammad's intercession as a means of salvation. *Sufi* Muslims take the mystical path, viewing salvation as loving and experiencing Allah and striving to become one with Allah.

Does salvation come by faith, works, or only by the sovereignty of Allah? Although Muslims do not believe that the nature of humanity needs to be changed, most agree that they must meet certain requirements for entrance into Paradise. Some insist that salvation comes only by faith. The collections of *Hadith* often refer to meritorious works, as seen in Al-Tirmidhi Hadith (Hadith 2):

I said to Allah's Messenger (peace be upon him): Inform me about an act which would entitle me to get into Paradise, and remove me away from Hell-Fire. He (the Prophet) said: You have asked me about a matter (which ostensibly appears to be) difficult but it is easy to those for whom Allah, the Exalted, has made it easy. Worship Allah and do not associate anything with him, establish prayer, pay the Zakat, observe the fast of Ramadan and perform Hajj to the (sacred) House (Ka'bah). He again said: Should I not direct you to the gateways of good? Listen to me: The fasting is a shield against evil, the charity extinguishes (the fire of sin) just as water extinguishes fire.[17]

---

[17] Al-Tirmidhi, Hadith 2, Alim.org,ttp://www.alim.org/library/hadith/pdf/ TIR/2, 1.

For some Muslims, refraining from polytheism earns salvation, while other Muslims believe that if a person does not commit *shirk*, an entrance to Paradise will be obtained. According to one *Hadith*, assurance of salvation comes only by dying in defense of Islam:

> Narrated Abu Huraira: The Prophet said, 'The person who participates in (holy battles) Allah's cause and nothing compels him to do so except belief in Allah and His Apostles, will be recompensed by Allah either with a reward, or booty (if he survives) or will be admitted to Paradise (if he is killed in the battle as a martyr). Had I not found it difficult for my followers, then I would not remain behind any *sariya* going for jihad and I would have loved to be martyred in Allah's cause and then made alive, and then martyred and then made alive, and then again martyred in His cause.'[18]

Biblical Truth Regarding Salvation

"Salvation is deliverance from spiritual death and enslavement by sin. God provides salvation for all who believe and accept His free offer of forgiveness. Mankind's only hope of redemption from the fallen sinful state is through the blood of Jesus Christ, God's son—blood that was shed as Jesus died on the cross."[19]

Jesus answered him, "Truly, truly, I say to you, unless one is born again, he cannot see the kingdom of God." (John 3:3)

For "everyone who calls on the name of the Lord will be saved." (Romans 10:13)

For by grace you have been saved through faith. And this is not your own doing; it is the gift of God, not a result of works, so that no one may boast. (Ephesians 2:8-9)

---

[18] Shakir Nasif Al-Ubaydi, Mahmud Hamad Nasr, and Muhammad Taqiy-ad-Din Al-Hilali, eds., *The Translation of the Meanings of Sahih Al-Bukhari,* vol.1, trans. Muhammad Muhsin Khan (Al-Medina: Islamic University, n.d.,) 38. *Sariya* is "a small army unit sent by the Prophet for *jihad* without his participation in it."

[19] Bicket, "Our 16 Doctrines," 6.

Prayer

Lord Jesus, Thank You for salvation that fully impacts every area of my life. Thank You that it is free. I realize that nothing I have done or can do would earn salvation for me. I am a recipient of divine biblical grace and mercy. Help me to live a life that testifies to this wonderful and amazing gift that continues to manifest itself within me.

WHAT MUSLIMS PRACTICE

The Quran and *Hadith* oblige Muslims to submit to Allah's will. Religion *(din)* refers to the human response to those obligations. The classical listing of the Pillars of Islam includes five devotional practices.

Muslims bear witness to the faith in fulfillment of their first duty. They publicly say, "I bear witness that there is no god but Allah, and Muhammad is the messenger of Allah." They refer to this as the confession of faith or *shahada.* Although the Quran does not contain these exact words, if a person says and believes these words, he or she becomes a Muslim.

Muslims sense the extreme importance of prayer *(salat)*. They perform the second aspect of Muslim devotion five times daily. Prayer represents submission to Allah. Prostration represents surrender while the required number of daily occurrences keeps the believer in remembrance of Allah. Muslims pay strict observance to purification and cleansing, thus symbolizing the need for cleansing the heart.

Muslims fast during *Ramadan*, the ninth month of the Muslim calendar. During daylight hours they consume neither food nor water, nor do they engage in sexual intercourse. The fast (*sawm*) focuses upon magnifying Allah and giving thanks. *Ramadan* obliges all Muslims to fast except for those who are under twelve, the old, and the incapacitated. The sick, pregnant women, travelers, and those in danger may postpone the fast, but they should try to make it up.

The fourth pillar of Islam, almsgiving (*zakat*), is required charity. The Caliph Umar said: "Prayer carries us half-way to Allah, fasting brings us to the door of his palace, and alms procures us admission."[20] This exemplifies the Islamic idea of salvation by works because Muslims understand them as expiation of sins.

The fifth pillar requires Muslims who are healthy and can afford it to make the pilgrimage (*hajj*) to Mecca. The *hajj* represents the apex of spiritual experience for Muslims. Islam carefully prescribes the procedures and rituals, and they provide enormous significance and symbolism for the pilgrim.

These five pillars of Islamic duty complete the classical list. Although some identify holy war (*jihad*) as the sixth pillar, many Muslims, especially in the West, seldom include it because of the negative connotation of violence associated with it. The *Hans Wehr Dictionary of Modern Written Arabic* defines the root of *jihad* as "exertion, endeavor, attempt, effort, trouble, pains."[21] Used with the appropriate preposition, it can mean to struggle or exert oneself on behalf of or for the sake of someone or something. Muslims understand *jihad* as striving in the way of Allah or striving to overcome evil. They struggle for moral and intellectual improvement. Muslims refer to the moral and ethical aspect as

---

[20] John C. Blair, *The Sources of Islam: An Inquiry into the Sources of the Faith and Practice of the Muhammadan Religion*, The Christian Literature Society for India (Madras, India: Allahabad, Rangoon, Colombo, 1925), accessed April 25, 2019, http://www.muhammadanism.org/blair/sources/blair_sources.pdf, 145.

[21] J. M. Cowan, ed., *The Hans Wehr Dictionary of Modern Written Arabic*, s.v. "Jihad," accessed April 25, 2019, https://bit.ly/2VrVaAk.

greater *jihad*, but they defend their religion by righteous war or lesser *jihad*. Most Muslims justify the use of violence only when all possible means to solve the problem have been exhausted.

FOLK ISLAM/
POPULAR ISLAM

In most monotheistic religions, a dichotomy develops between faith, as defined in theology, and faith, as expressed in the believers' lives. Many of the world's Muslims are involved in magic, witchcraft, and other occult practices. A Muslim may affirm orthodox belief, practice the pillars of faith, and yet deviate from orthodoxy by emphasizing local customs and heartfelt needs. Folk Islam attempts to solve the problems of life through animistic practices rather than through formal religion, focusing on life crises such as disease, famine, war, and death. Unlike formal organizations, Folk Islam never institutionalized. Authority rests in the practitioner's proven power rather than in his or her official position. The practices of Folk Muslims are not canonized in written form. They preserve their beliefs and practices in myth and ritual, and they pass them on to future generations by word of mouth.

The movement gains popularity by focusing on people and their needs, and the rites of worship center on local saints and shrines. Although formal Islam restricts women from certain religious activities, Folk Islam allows them to openly perform the local rituals of popular religion in search of blessing (*baraka*) and power. Consequently, Folk Islam is particularly attractive to women.

Orthodox Muslims honor Muhammad as the Prophet of Islam, but Folk Muslims venerate him as a power figure, and it seems that Muhammad himself encouraged the practice. A tradition relates that Muhammad equated faith in Islam with love for him that surpasses the natural love for one's family. It seems that Muhammad was borrowing from the words of Jesus: *"Anyone who loves their father or mother more than me is not worthy of me; anyone who loves their son or daughter more than me is not worthy of me"* (Matthew 10:37). Jesus could say this because He was the Son of God, but Muhammad could make no such claim of divinity.

Folk Muslims name mosques and shrines after their heroes, including Muhammad. Muslims believe that saints possess power even after death, and Muslims visit their shrines and gravesites as part of their worship. Pilgrims seek power, *baraka*, and direct answers to prayer. In formal Islam, believers pray memorized corporate prayers in mosques. They often pray in Arabic without understanding the words. Folk Islam, on the other hand, allows one to pray heart-felt prayers to saints in their own local dialect. They fear the unknown, the future, evil, and sickness. They attempt to manipulate spiritual forces through persons, objects, places, and rituals. Lack of connectedness to community causes shame and perceived powerlessness against evil. Folk Muslims seek meaning to life and death and secrets to success. For them, reality means the evil eye, superstition, curses, fetishes, talismans, charms, magic, idolatry, spirits, and the petitioning of saints or angels for *baraka*.

Folk practices often become part of one's faith as a carryover from paganism to formal religion. For example, syncretism threatens Christian missionary endeavors in parts of the world. People accept the claims of the Bible and even take part in water baptism, yet they continue to participate in animistic practices. Although foreign to biblical Christian life, these customs and habits cling like barnacles. However, the Quran and *Hadith* actually encourage such practices in Islam. The teachings, practices, and sayings of Muhammad give precedence for invoking the saints, using supernatural curses, visiting and circumambulating the shrines of saints, kissing the black stone in Mecca, and drinking holy water from the well of *Zamzam* in Mecca for *baraka* and healing. Thus, animism inherently resides in Islam.

Muslims even use passages from the Quran as supernatural remedies. They find more value in the mystical power of the Quran than in its meaning. Reciting or writing holy words invokes power over evil, even though they may not understand the Arabic words. A practitioner writes the holy words on paper, puts the paper in a charm, and gives it to someone to wear for protection. Sometimes the practitioner writes them on a chalkboard and then dusts the chalk into a glass of water to drink as a magic potion. Phil Parshall explains how Folk Muslims use the Quran:

> Sura 113 is believed to be a deterrent to all sorts of disease. Sura 114 has the power to counteract psychic afflictions. Suras 94 and 105 are to be recited early in the morning as a safeguard against toothaches. Sura 72 is to be quoted when one is fearful of the power of evil jinn. Sura 13 is a cure for headaches.[22]

Ordinary Muslims live in a context in which the spirit world plays a major part, and only supernatural help controls the spiritual powers. Formal religion does not meet their needs.

Islam emphasizes law, ritual, and duty. Sufism, a mystical sect of Islam, "stresses emotions, feelings, the personal attributes of Allah, personal relations with Allah, love, and heartfelt religion."[23] Sufis attempt to revitalize formal religion. They seek intimacy and union with Allah through vigorous worship and piety. Worshipers pray, sing, chant, and move their bodies by swaying, twirling, or other physical motions. They want experience and feeling in their

---

[22] Phil Parshall, *Bridges to Islam: A Christian Perspective on Folk Islam* (Downers Grove, IL: InterVarsity Press, 2007), 75.

[23] George W. Braswell, *Islam: Its Prophet, Politics, and Power* (Nashville, TN: Broadman and Holman, 1996), 19.

religion. Orthodox Muslims view Folk Islam, including Sufism, as heresy.

People who seek answers to real life problems through folk religion will not find satisfaction through formal religion of any kind. Christian discipleship must not merely replace one theological system with another. Spiritual transformation brings people into relationship with a living God who interacts with them. Converts from Islam must learn to trust God for their needs.

Prayer

Lord Jesus, I choose to believe Your Word for "Your Word is truth" (John 17:17). My enemy is Satan, the Devil, the deceiver, the accuser of the believer, and the father of lies. Jesus, Your Word tells me that the Son of God appeared to destroy the works of the devil (1 John 3:8). I recognize and hold to the fact that You have accomplished everything necessary to assist me in life. I also believe You are and always will be my source of help and strength, according to Psalm 146.

FAMILY TIES, COMMUNITY, AND CELEBRATIONS

Islamic community (*umma*) directs morals, mores, and cultural institutions. The Quran and the life of the Prophet provide the manual and pattern for family life, social structure, and community. Although theological identification provides the basis of affiliation, family serves as the basic unit of society, and most activities revolve around the family. Reputation and honor come from family, and violations of unwritten codes cause shame, generate strong negative feelings, and elicit emotional responses.

With few exceptions, mostly due to westernization and emigration, Muslims often live with their extended families. If not in the same building, they live in close proximity. Although not unique to Muslims, the principle of the extended family is common in Muslim cultures even under the pressures of modern society and globalization. Extended families share responsibilities in childrearing, and Muslim rites of passage take place within that context. Family affiliation provides social security, economic support, emotional undergirding, physical maintenance, and decision-making for all members. The head of the family, and in some cases the oldest son, makes decisions for other children, especially in the areas of education and marriage. Although families that have emigrated may live as a nuclear family, their support base usually remains the extended family in their country of origin.

Second to theological convictions, family provides the glue of Islamic community. The family serves as a person's ultimate refuge. Most Muslims would not want to risk being disowned by their family. Feelings resulting from social ties may be intangible, but they are powerful. How can you, as a new believer, appeal to the church to become your new community? Spiritual transformation seeks an answer to this important question.

Islamic festivals and celebrations create feelings of identification for Muslims. Holidays and religious observances follow the lunar calendar, which dates from the *Hegira*, the day of Muhammad's flight from Mecca to Medina in A.D. 622.[24] Some holidays call for festive celebrations while others create a more somber atmosphere. Some are universal while others are local.

The Tenth of Muharram

Muharram is the first month of the Muslim lunar calendar. Some know the holiday as Ashura. All Muslims commemorate Muharram as a day of mourning. *Sunnis* remember all martyrs; *Shia* especially remember Ali, Muhammad's son-in-law, and the grandsons of the Prophet, Hasan and Husain, who were killed by Sunnis. On that date in the year A.D. 680, *Sunnis* and *Shia* battled over the leadership issue.

Maulid al-Nabi

Maulid al-Nabi or *Milaad al-Nabi* means the "Birthday of the Prophet," and it occurs on the twelfth of the third month. Some Muslims engage in excessive veneration of the Prophet. Orthodox

---

[24] See Appendix for more information on the lunar calendar and annual celebrations.

Muslims disapprove of too much festivity, cautioning against anything that removes emphasis from Allah.

Mi'raj

Mi'raj celebrates Muhammad's Night Journey on a winged animal from Mecca to al-Aqsa Mosque in Jerusalem where he ascended to heaven and then returned to Mecca the same night. *Mi'raj* literally means "an ascent." While in heaven, Muhammad ventured near the throne of Allah. Sufis find symbolism in *Mi'raj* for their quest to encounter the divine. Most information comes from *Hadith* as only one verse in the Quran refers to the Night Journey, and it does not mention the ascension (Quran 17:1).

Lailat al Bara'a

Lailat al Bara'a, or Night of Repentance, occurs on the fourteenth of the eighth month. Not mentioned in the Quran, tradition teaches that Allah descends to the lowest heaven on this night to call people to repentance and to grant forgiveness for sins. The festivities often resemble New Year's celebrations.

Lailat al-Qadar

Lailat al-Qadar, or Night of Power, occurs on the 27th of Ramadan, the next to the last night of the month of fasting. It commemorates the night when Muhammad received the first revelation. Muslims have great expectations for answered prayer, many spending the entire evening in prayer.

Id al-Fitr

Muslims celebrate on the first of the tenth month of the Muslim calendar, marking the breaking of the fast. The festivities last two to three days; during this time people may visit cemeteries in respect for the dead. Considered the lesser of the two major festivals, it is the most spontaneously joyful of all celebrations.

Id al-Adha

Considered as their major festival, the Feast of Sacrifice, or the Great Feast, falls on the tenth of the twelfth month of the calendar, marking the end of the pilgrimage. Lasting several days, the festival commemorates the sacrificing of an animal in place of Abraham's son, believed by Muslims to have been Ishmael.

Islamic community, primarily the family, maintains tremendous influence over the individual. Many Muslims would hardly make an important decision without consulting family. Family and community relationships are impacted by a CMB's decision to follow Christ. Consequently, one should not underestimate the weight of what CMBs leave behind as a result of their newfound Christian faith. However, there is much to be gained!

It is our prayer that Part Two of this book will be a helpful guide to the new believer throughout the process of discipleship. Let us turn now to Part 2, "Your Pentecostal Journey to Maturity."

Part 2

Your Pentecostal Journey to Maturity

DISCIPLESHIP
LESSONS

The following course contains ten lessons. Each lesson will include sidebar questions to aid the disciple in thinking through various facets of his or her own Christian journey. At the beginning of each lesson, we also introduce Tahir, a believer in Christ from a Muslim background. He is a Spirit-filled believer who has faithfully served the Lord for over 20 years. Tahir's story may help you apply the teachings in each chapter.

Lesson 1, "Your New Guide," presents the Bible as the disciple's new guide. The first chapter of the Quran is a prayer for guidance that Muslims pray believing it will keep them on the right path that leads to Allah's mercy, not to his judgment. They believe that they obtain guidance (*hidiyaat*) in Allah's revelation, the Quran. Muslims do not believe that they need redemption but that they need guidance to keep them from stumbling. For them, the Quran reveals Allah's will and law, not his character. Lesson 1 presents the Bible as God's self-revelation that guides people to right relationship with Him. While Muslims believe that the Quran was sent down in the same form that it exists in heaven, Christians believe that the Holy Spirit inspired writers and they communicated God's message. Christians further believe that as the Bible is the written Word of God, Jesus Christ is the Living Word of God.

Lesson 2, "Your New Lord," compares and contrasts the God of the Bible with the god/Allah of the Quran. The Bible presents God as one and transcendent. However, unlike the god/Allah of the Quran, the God of the Bible reveals himself in three persons, God the Father, God the Son, and God the Holy Spirit. Unlike the Quran, the Bible portrays God not only as transcendent but also as immanent.

Lesson 3, "Your New Friend," introduces Jesus as the believer's friend (John 15:15) and gives some biblical titles for Jesus. Passages from the Gospels, Hebrews, and Colossians inform disciples concerning the nature of Christ. A study of selected passages from Hebrews and Philippians provides instruction on the incarnation, *kenosis*, and sacrificial atonement. Moses and the prophets foretold of the coming of Christ, and the New Testament teaches that Jesus will come again to take His followers to be with Him forever.

Lesson 4, "Your New Path, Part One," describes the believer's new life as a follower of Christ. The Quran uses the word *path* in Surah 1 to mean the Muslim's way to Allah's will. This lesson describes the disciple's way to new life in Christ. Since Muslims and Christians understand sin differently, the study articulates the biblical position on the sinful nature of humanity, explains the biblical path to salvation, and enumerates the benefits of salvation.

Lesson 5, "Your New Path, Part Two," describes the disciple's continuation along the path toward God. Addressing the subject of discipleship, the lesson articulates the biblical concepts of self-denial, cross-bearing, and following Christ. The disciplined life focuses on Bible study, prayer, fellowship, ministry, and fruit-bearing.

Lesson 6, "Your New Helper, Part One," introduces the person, deity, and work of the Holy Spirit to the new believer. The Quran states that only a little information about the Holy Spirit (*Ruh al-*

Qudus) has been given to Muhammad (Quran 17:85). If Muhammad was mistaken about the person of Christ, he had no idea concerning the Holy Spirit! The same Spirit who empowered individuals in the Old Testament, anointed Jesus, emboldened the early believers, and helps disciples today. He empowers believers for service, exalts Christ, and teaches believers concerning Jesus.

Lesson 7, "Your New Helper, Part Two," provides further instruction about the Holy Spirit by explaining Pentecostal beliefs, such as the baptism in the Holy Spirit, empowerment for service, and speaking in tongues. By furnishing biblical grounds, the lesson encourages disciples to receive the fullness of the Spirit and gives practical advice on receiving the Pentecostal experience.

Lesson 8, "Your New Community, Part One," informs the disciple concerning his or her new community found in the church. Islam provides community for Muslims. When a Muslim becomes a follower of Christ, the Islamic community might ostracize him or her, and former social and economic associations might cease. The church becomes the disciple's new family and community. By looking at Paul's metaphors for the church, Lesson 8 addresses the church's nature and its obligation to believers as well as non-believers. Membership in the new community has privileges as well as responsibilities.

Lesson 9, "Your New Community, Part Two," considers the subjects of worship, the ordinances of the Church, and spiritual gifts for ministry. This course does not attempt a thorough examination of the doctrine of the Church.

Lesson 10, "Your New Struggle," addresses the subject of spiritual warfare. Although it has been interpreted variously, the basic Islamic understanding of *jihad* refers to a Muslim's individual struggle against evil. This lesson puts that struggle into a Christian context. The study first identifies the enemy, who is not flesh and blood but the devil. Although Muslims attempt many methods of achieving spiritual power in order to overcome evil powers, the disciple learns that only Jesus possesses true authority over the enemy, and Jesus freely gives that authority to His disciples.

Jesus commanded the Church to *"make disciples of all nations"* (Matthew 28:19). This simple command has tremendous implications. The Church must baptize new believers (v. 19), as well as teach them to obey all the teachings of Jesus (v. 20). The passage emphasizes that disciples come from all nations (v. 19). This relevant passage not only underscores the universal nature of the gospel and missions, but stresses the differences of people groups. Discipleship of former Muslims must consider this crucial reality. Since Muslims make up 20 percent of the world's population, and since the differences between Muslims and Christians are so pronounced, Christian discipleship must target problem areas with biblical truth.

Thorough discipleship forms Christ in CMBs and assists them to endure the pressures that Islamic society puts upon those who choose to leave Islam. Executed properly, discipleship forms disciples who will reproduce themselves. Groups of mature disciples form churches that stand the test of time. Such indigenous churches survive in hostile societies. Totalitarian regimes, religious bigotry, financial hardship, and persecution cannot destroy the true Church. Jesus promised, *"I will build my church, and the gates of hell shall not prevail against it"* (Matthew 16:18) and discipleship is the method Jesus has chosen to build His Church.

Tahir's Story

"Tahir, do you still have the Bible I gave you?" asked John, as he sat next to his friend. Tahir had just given his life to Christ.

"Sure do! I've skimmed some of it, but now I'm looking forward to reading all of it!"

"Let me encourage you to read it every day," continued John "It's God's Word for you."

"Should I just start at the beginning and read it through?" inquired the new believer.

"I would suggest that everyday you read at least one chapter from Psalms, one chapter from Proverbs, one additional chapter from the Old Testament as well as one chapter from the New Testament. Reading this way will give you a great understanding of various sections of the Bible. As you read, ask God to speak to you from His Word."

"Sounds great, John. I'm looking forward to reading something I can actually understand."

"What do you mean?"

"Well, I'm from Pakistan, so Arabic is not my mother-tongue, though I know some words. All my life I've been reciting the Quran without really understanding it. Now, I'll be able to read the Bible with understanding."

From the beginning of his conversion to Christ, Tahir had a love for the Word of God. He poured over its pages like someone who had just found a hidden treasure. As he grew in Christ, he began talking to others about making the Bible their guide for life. Later, Tahir enrolled in a Bible college to study the Bible intensively.

Lesson 1
Your New Guide

*"Your word is a lamp to my feet and a light
to my path."* (Psalm 119:105)[25]

As a new follower of Jesus (*Isa*) you have put your faith in Him to guide you on the right path. This does not mean that you now have a new list of things to do and not do. What it does mean is that Jesus has paid the price for you to be acceptable in God's sight. The new path is not a path of law but a path of grace. This is not to say that God did not give laws for His people to obey. But He has also provided enough grace to enable His people to live according to His expectations. God has put you on the right path, and now you trust Him to keep you on that path. Later we will look at how God put you on that path and what that path is. Now, we want to look closer at the guide.

---

[25] All scriptural quotations are from the English Standard Version, unless otherwise noted.

We believe that the Bible is the written Word of God. As God's Word, the Bible is our rule of faith and conduct. We do not believe that God "sent down" his will or law while remaining separate and unknown. Neither did God dictate His law.

In your own words, how did God give His Word to the human race?

1. 2 Peter 1:21

2. 2 Timothy 3:16-17

Inspiration means that God breathed His Holy Spirit into men and women so that they were moved to record His revelation accurately and without error. God did not use people like a typewriter or a dictation machine. We believe that God's Holy Spirit used their personalities, styles, education, and experiences so that they wrote precisely what God wanted them to write. The Holy Spirit directed the authorship of Scripture. Even though the Bible was written over a period of 1,500 years by at least 40 authors from different backgrounds, it displays miraculous unity.

How has the Word of God impacted your life since you became a Christian?

As you read Scripture, look for words that are used to mean "God's message." Any references to Scripture, the law of the Lord, statutes, Word of God, decrees, commands, precepts, teachings, and so forth should be understood as portions or the complete Bible. The Bible is revelation. God reveals himself and His law to humankind.

What can nature teach us about God?

3. Psalm 19:1-4

4. Romans 1:18-20

Nature provides general revelation, but to understand God's plan of salvation and to know His will for us, we need special revelation. God is indeed transcendent (separate from His creation), but He is also immanent. He communicates by interacting in history.

How does God communicate in the following verses?

5. Deuteronomy 11:2-7

6. 1 Samuel 3:21

7. 1 Samuel 12:6-7

8. Romans 16:25-27

What is the purpose of revelation?

9. Psalm 1:1-6

10. John 8:31-32

11. 1 Corinthians 10:11

12. 1 Corinthians 15:4

13. 2 Timothy 3:15

14. 2 Timothy 3:16-17

15. Romans 15:4

16. Romans 16:25

17. Hebrews 4:12-13

In the previous Scripture verses you learned that revelation provides examples for instruction, gives wisdom, makes disciples, reveals truth, gives freedom, leads to salvation, teaches, reproves, corrects, trains, prophesies, predicts, shows how prophecy is fulfilled, gives hope, and establishes you. In other words, Scripture produces disciples. It forms Christ in you (Galatians 4:19). We could sum this up by saying that the Bible is our guide. Since the Bible conveys God's message, it carries the same authority as if

God spoke to you personally. Therefore, it is important that as a disciple you read God's message daily. Study the Bible and commit as many Scriptures to memory as possible.

Satan tempted Jesus to turn stones into bread to satisfy His hunger. Jesus responded by quoting Deuteronomy 8:3: *"It is written, 'Man shall not live by bread alone, but by every word that comes from the mouth of God'"* (Matthew 4:4). Think of God's words as spiritual food. As the body needs food every day, the spirit also requires daily sustenance. We cannot grow unless we have a healthy diet. We can ingest the Word in several ways. Listen to anointed biblical preaching, read the Bible, study it, memorize it, meditate upon it, and most importantly, apply it. If you do not already have a habit of daily prayer and Bible study, begin setting a certain block of time aside each day to pray, read the Bible, and meditate on what God is saying to you from the Bible. Always keep a journal handy so you can write down your observations. Ask questions about what you read in Scripture. What was God's message for that situation in the Bible? How does it apply today? Write down what you think God is saying to you.

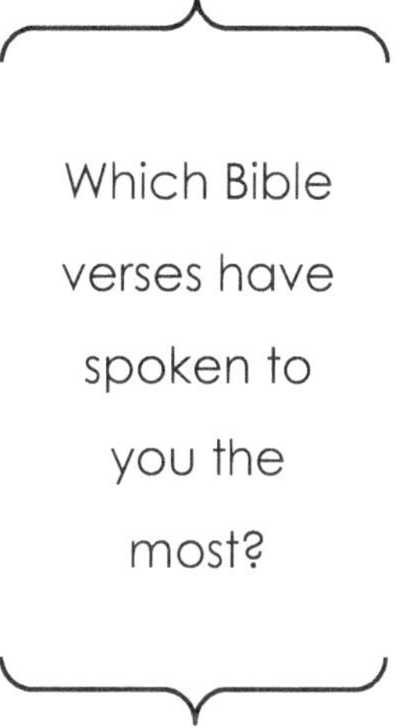

As the Bible is the "Written Word" of God, Jesus Christ is the "Living Word" of God. What does the Bible say about Jesus Christ as God's revelation?

18. John 1:1-18

19. 2 Corinthians 4:6

20. Hebrews 1:1-3

21. John 14:6-7

22. Matthew 11:27

The way to have the Living Word in our lives is to live in the Word. Christ lives in us when His Word is in us. *"Then said Jesus to those Jews which believed on him, 'If ye continue in my word, then are ye my disciples indeed; And ye shall know the truth, and the truth shall make you free'"* (John 8:31-32, KJV). To continue in the Word also means to obey it. The New International Version (NIV) reads, *"To the Jews who had believed him, Jesus said, 'If you hold to my teaching, you are really my disciples'"* (John 8:31).

23. What metaphor does Paul use to describe the Word of God as part of an arsenal of spiritual weapons (Ephesians 6:11-18)?

24. Memory Verses

All Scripture is breathed out by God and profitable for teaching, for reproof, for correction, and for training in righteousness, that the man of God may be complete, equipped for every good work. (2 Timothy 3:16)

For no prophecy was ever produced by the will of man, but men spoke from God as they were carried along by the Holy Spirit. (2 Peter 1:21)

Your word is a lamp to my feet and a light to my path. (Psalm 119:105)

25. Action Steps

Read Psalm 119. Reflect on each section. Take a pen and notebook and write down all of the benefits of the Word of God. Notice all the terms used to mean God's Word.

26. Rethink the Lesson

- God inspired prophets, apostles, and others to write Scripture.

- The Bible is God's written Word.

- The Bible is God's self-revelation.

- By reading, internalizing, and obeying the Word, we become Christ's disciples.

- The Bible is our guide.

Answers to Lesson 1

1. Men spoke from God as they were moved or carried along by the Holy Spirit.

2. God-breathed; inspired by God

3. The heavens declare the glory of God; the skies proclaim the work of His hands. They display knowledge and the voice of creation speaks about the greatness of God.

4. Creation reveals God's invisible qualities.

5. They saw and experienced the discipline of the Lord with their own eyes.

6. He revealed himself to Samuel through His word.

7. He performed righteous acts.

8. Through prophetic writings

9. Revelation establishes, matures, strengthens, and produces fruit.

10. The reader will know the truth and the truth will set him or her free.

11. Examples and warnings

12. Fulfill the Scriptures

13. It makes the disciple wise for salvation through faith in Christ Jesus.

14. Teaching, rebuking, correcting, and training in righteousness

15. Teach and encourage

16. Establishes the disciple

17. Penetrates and judges

18. He is the Word; He was with God; He was God; He was with God in the beginning; He was the true Light; He gave people power to become the sons of God; the Word became flesh and made His dwelling among us; He came from the Father; He brought grace and truth; and He makes known the Father.

19. He is the light that gives us the knowledge of the glory of God.

20. God speaks in these last days through His Son. He is the radiance of God's glory and the exact representation of His being.

21. Way, Truth, and the Life

22. The Son reveals the Father.

23. Sword of the Spirit

Tahir's Story

"I'm so happy for you, Tahir," said John, as he and his former Muslim friend sat at the front of the church. "You've taken a huge step in giving your life to Christ."

"Thanks," said Tahir, still wiping away tears from his eyes. "All my life, I've wanted to experience the presence of God. Now I have."

"Tahir, you can experience God's presence every day. He is close to you and wants a relationship with you."

At that, more tears started flowing down Tahir's face. For a long time prior to coming to Christ, Tahir felt spiritually empty. Despite doing all that Islam required of him, God still seemed far away. He longed for God, but didn't know how to get to Him.

The idea of a personal God seemed too good to be true to Tahir. As Tahir grew in his faith, he longed to tell others about his Heavenly Father.

Lesson 2
Your New Lord

"God is Spirit, and those who worship him must worship in spirit and truth." (John 4:24)

As a follower of Jesus, you are gaining a new understanding of who God is and what He is like. In the first lesson, you learned that God has revealed himself in the book we call the Bible. God is a self-revealing God. This lesson will teach you some things God has revealed about himself. Some Muslims say Christians worship three gods. Is this true?

What does the Bible teach us about God?

1. Deuteronomy 6:4-5

2. Isaiah 43:10-11

3. **Mark 12:29-30**

4. **John 4:21-24**

5. **Acts 17:24-25**

6. **God is the creator and sustainer of all things. How did He create all things (Genesis 1:1-31)?**

7. **Why did God create the heavens (Scripture is speaking here of the heavenly bodies, sun, moon, stars, etc.) and earth (Isaiah 45:18-19)?**

Although the term Trinity is not found in the Bible, Christians use the word to express the biblical concept that the One true God reveals himself as a plurality within unity: God the Father, God the Son, and God the Holy Spirit.

8. **Jesus instructed His disciples to baptize believers in what name (Matthew 28:19)?**

The Apostle Paul ended his second letter to the Corinthians by praying this benediction: *"The grace of the Lord Jesus Christ and the love of God and the fellowship of the Holy Spirit be with you all"* (2 Corinthians 13:14).

9. At the baptism of Jesus, something extraordinary occurred. What was it (Luke 3:22)?

10. Do you think this was significant? Why?

11. What did Jesus say about His relationship with God (John 10:25-30)?

12. Why did the Jews want to stone Jesus (John 10:31-33)?

Note the cooperation of the Father, Jesus Christ, and the Spirit.

13. 1 Peter 1:1-3

14. Jude 20-21

Since God is infinite and our minds are finite, it should be no surprise that no one can fully explain the mystery of the Triune God that is presented in the Bible The One true God has revealed himself in three persons: Father, Son (Jesus Christ), and Holy Spirit.

Concerning mankind's relationship with God, Christians believe in transcendence, or distance. This means that God distances himself from creation, and it refers to God's superiority over creation. *"For as the heavens are higher than the earth, so are my ways higher than your ways and my thoughts than your thoughts"* (Isaiah 55:9). *"Who is like the Lord our God, who is seated on high, who looks far down on the heavens and the earth"* (Psalm 113:5-6)? Christians also believe in immanence, or nearness. This refers to God's presence in the world and His interaction with creation.

How near is God to humanity?

15. Job 27:3

16. Genesis 2:7

What do the prophets have to say about the Spirit of God in relation to immanence?

As your Heavenly Father, how has God taken care of you?

17. Isaiah 63:11

18. Haggai 2:5

19. How close does Paul portray Jesus Christ to His disciples (Colossians 1:27-28)?

20. How close does Paul say God is to all people (Acts 17:22-28)?

Not only does the Bible teach immanence, but it describes God as love: *"Anyone who does not love does not know God, because God is love"* (1 John 4:8). Paul refers to God as *"the God of love and peace"* (2 Corinthians 13:11).

To whom does God demonstrate His benevolence?

21. Matthew 5:45

22. Psalm 145:16

23. Why did God give His Son, Jesus, to die on the cross (John 3:16)?

24. God's love has made us _______ __ _______ (1 John 3:1).

25. Memory Verses

For God so loved the world that he gave his only Son, that whoever believes in him should not perish but have eternal life. (John 3:16)

In the beginning, God created the heavens and the earth. (Genesis 1:1)

Go therefore and make disciples of all nations, baptizing them in the name of the Father and of the Son and of the Holy Spirit. (Matthew 28:19)

26. Action Steps

The Bible reveals God's character to us. Christian theologians refer to His characteristics as attributes. Look up the references in your Bible for the following attributes. Reflect on the meanings. In addition to transcendence, immanence, and love, God is:

- Holy (Isaiah 41:14; 57:15; Acts 3:14; Ephesians 4:30)

- Self-existent (John 5:26; 1 Timothy 6:16)

- Eternal (Psalm 90:2; Habakkuk 1:12; Hebrews 1:10-12)

- Just or righteous (Deuteronomy 10:17-18; Psalm 116:5; 145:17; Hebrews 6:10)

- Merciful (Psalm 103:8; Luke 6:36)

- Unchanging (Malachi 3:6; Hebrews 13:8; James 1:17)

- Omnipresent (He is present everywhere) (Psalm 139:7-12; Jeremiah 23:23-24)

- Omniscient (all-knowing) (Job 11:7-8; Psalm 147:5; Romans 11:33)

- Omnipotent (all-powerful) (Genesis 1:1-2; Job 42:2; Daniel 4:35; James 4:12-15)

27. Rethink the Lesson

- The Bible teaches that God has revealed himself as one God in three persons.

- God created and sustains all things.

- Although God is high above all things, He is involved in the affairs of daily life.

- God is love.

- God is spirit.

- The Bible reveals God's character. God is holy, self-existent, eternal, just, merciful, unchanging, omnipresent, omniscient, and omnipotent.

Answers to Lesson 2

1. God is one.

2. There is no other God; there is no other Savior.

3. God is one, and He is to be loved and served completely.

4. God is Spirit.

5. God does not live in temples made with hands.

6. God spoke everything into existence.

7. God made the earth to be inhabited, and He did not speak in secret from a land of darkness, but His spectacular creation speaks truth and what is right. Therefore, people do not seek God in vain. His creation is revelation and communication.

8. In the name of the Father and of the Son and of the Holy Spirit

9. While Jesus was praying, the Holy Spirit descended in the form of a dove, and a voice came from heaven saying, *"You are my beloved Son; with you I am well pleased."*

10. Thus, in one verse, there is mention of the Son, the Holy Spirit, and although the voice is not identified as the Father, it is obvious that the voice is that of the Father.

11. I and the Father are one.

12. They wanted to stone Jesus for blasphemy for they said that He was a mere man claiming to be God.

13. The elect, had been chosen for obedience, or discipleship, to Christ and the sprinkling by His blood by the foreknowledge of God, through the sanctifying work of the Spirit.

14. Pray in the Holy Spirit, keep yourselves in the love of God, and wait for the mercy of the Lord Jesus Christ to bring you eternal life.

15. The breath of God was within Job.

16. God breathed the breath of life into Adam.

17. God brought the people through the sea, and He set His Holy Spirit among them.

18. The Lord encouraged Zerubbabel and Joshua by the prophet Haggai saying to them that His Spirit remains among them.

19. Christ was in them.

20. God is not far from each person. In Him we live and move and have our being. We are His offspring.

21. On the evil and on the good, and on the just and the unjust

22. Every living thing

23. God loves the world.

24. Children of God

Tahir's Story

"How could Allah have a son?" began Ahmad, Tahir's cousin. "That is impossible."

Tahir sat in his cousin's living room talking about Jesus over cups of tea. It had only been two weeks since he had given his life to Christ. Growing up in a Muslim family, Tahir highly respected Jesus as a prophet. However, when he first heard Christians declare that Jesus is God's Son, he bristled at the notion. Yet, after experiencing the love of Christians, he began to wonder if there was validity to their teaching. It was this love that began to break down the walls of Tahir's heart. Later, Tahir recognized that God had been drawing him to himself.

Tahir replied to his cousin, "All my life I prayed that God would show me the way to true life. Then I heard the voice of God telling me that Jesus *is* the way! I longed for a relationship with God, but there is no other way to Him except through Jesus. Nothing compares to experiencing God's love!"

When Tahir committed his life to Christ, he began to see Jesus as far more than a prophet. Indeed, this former Muslim came to see Jesus as the way, the truth, and the life, and he longed for people, like his cousin, Ahmad, to know Jesus in this way as well.

Lesson 3
Your New Friend

*No longer do I call you servants, for the servant does
not know what his master is doing; but I have called
you friends, for all that I have heard from
my Father I have made known to you.*
(John 15:15)

Jesus calls us friends because He has shared with us the greatest revelation of the ages. Abraham was called the friend of God because of his faith (James 2:23). The fact that Jesus is your best friend does not mean that He deserves any less respect and honor.

Note just some of the titles ascribed to Jesus in the Bible.

1. **Philippians 2:9-11**

2.   John 12:12-15

3.   Revelation 19:11-16

4.   Matthew 16:16; John 4:25-26

5.   Revelation 22:12-13

6.   Revelation 22:16

Christians believe Jesus Christ to be deity. Read the following passages: Do you think that they teach that Jesus possesses deity and that He is the Son of God?

7.   John 1:1-34

8.   Philippians 2:1-11

9.   Colossians 2:6-10

Jesus never explicitly claimed, "I am God." However, He made certain statements that could not have been made by someone less than God. He said that the angels, usually referred to as God's angels (Luke 12:8-9; 15:10), and the kingdom, usually referred to as the kingdom of God, belonged to Him (Matthew 13:41). Notice that Jesus' favorite title for himself was the "Son of Man." Furthermore, in the Sermon on the Mount, Jesus consistently sets himself up as superior to Moses and to the Law of Moses (Matthew 5-7; Luke 6:20-49).

In John's Gospel, Jesus understood His role as the judge of all mankind (John 5:22), and He explicitly declared that all would honor Him just as they honor the Father (v. 23). Jesus also states that the Scriptures testify about Him, and He strongly implies that one obtains eternal life only by coming to Him (v. 24). Jesus actually made a claim to preexistence: *Jesus said to them, 'Truly, truly, I say to you, before Abraham was, I am'"* (John 8:58).

How has your friendship with Jesus changed your life?

Jesus exercised His prerogative to forgive sins. At a Pharisee's house, a woman washed Jesus' feet with her tears, dried them with her hair, and poured expensive perfume on them. Jesus then forgave the woman's sins.

10. What was the reaction of the guests (Luke 7:36-49)?

11. Why did the Pharisees charge Jesus with blasphemy in Mark 2:5-10?

In the courts of the temple, the Pharisees brought to Jesus a woman who had been caught in the act of adultery. Jesus invited anyone who was sinless to cast the first stone. He did not condemn the woman, but He exhorted her to leave her life of sin (John 8:3-11).

12. Why did everyone, except Jesus, leave?

13. Hebrews 4:15 sheds some light on the story in John 8. What does it reveal?

As God's Son, Jesus has a special relationship with the Father and a special role in creation.

14. What is Jesus' special relationship with the Father (Hebrews 1:2)?

15. Notice the Son's role in creation (Hebrews 1:2).

The Son is the *"radiance of God's glory"* as the ray is the light of the sun (Hebrews 1:3). Verse 3 says that Jesus is *"the exact representation of his* [God's] *being."*

16. In Colossians 1:15, Paul says that Jesus Christ is the *"image of the* _________________________.

Notice that *"the firstborn of all creation,"* in Colossians 1:15, does not mean that Jesus was the first one created. It means that, as heir and like all first-born sons, he has certain privileges, rights, and authority over creation. Jesus is not merely a reflection of deity; He is the exact, authentic representation of God's essence.

God not only created the universe, He sustains it. He is not completely separate from the world and the creatures that He created. The so-called "laws of nature" have been established and they operate by God's decree.

17. How is nature, i.e., all of creation, sustained (Hebrews 1:3)?

Although the passage does not explain exactly how He accomplished it, the writer to the Hebrews mentions God's way for taking care of humanity's sin problem

18. The Son provided (Hebrews 1:3)__________________.

Christians believe that the vicarious atonement of Christ provided salvation from judgment, deliverance from the power of sin and death, and acceptance by God. Jesus understood it as His mission. His sacrifice distinguishes Christianity from all other religions. Jesus explained that all the Scriptures predicted His suffering:

> *And* [Jesus] *said to them, "Thus it is written, that the Christ should suffer and on the third day rise from the dead, and that repentance for the forgiveness of sins should be proclaimed in his name to all nations, beginning from Jerusalem.* (Luke 24:46-47)

19. Why did Jesus come to earth in the form of a human being (Luke 19:10)?

The process by which Jesus came to earth in the form of a human being is called the incarnation.

20. How would He accomplish His mission (Matthew 20:28)?

The author of Hebrews writes about the incarnation. Read the entire second chapter of Hebrews. *"Therefore he had to be made like his brothers in every respect"* (Hebrews 2:17). List three reasons for the incarnation from Hebrews 2:16-18.

21. Hebrews 2:17

22. Hebrews 2:17

23. Hebrews 2:18

Notice the reference to the earthly existence of Christ:

In the days of his flesh, Jesus offered up prayers and supplications, with loud cries and tears, to him who was able to save him from death, and he was heard because of his reverence. (Hebrews 5:7)

The sacrificial death of Christ gave purpose and meaning to the incarnation. Only God himself could provide the perfect sacrifice for sin. There can be no doubt that Jesus possessed a consciousness of both His identity and His mission.

We have studied the purpose of the incarnation. Now let us take a closer look at what the incarnation was and what it meant. First, look at Philippians 2:6-11.

24. What was Christ's nature (Philippians 2:6)?

25. Christ was equal to whom (Philippians 2:6)?

26. What nature did he take on (Philippians 2:7)?

27. What likeness and appearance did he assume (Philippians 2:7-8)?

Christ humbled himself, becoming obedient to death, not just any death, but to death on a cross. Death by crucifixion was for the worst criminals; it was degrading, humiliating, and excruciatingly painful. Jesus suffered immensely. As the pure and holy Son of God, He left heaven, humbled himself, and became nothing (Philippians 2:7). As shown earlier, He did it to supply the sacrifice for the sins of humanity. God exalted Jesus because of His obedience.

28. What did God do in response to Jesus' obedience, even to the point of death upon a cross (Philippians 2:9)?

29. The name of Jesus is________________________ (Philippians 2:9).

30. At the name of Jesus, what will everyone do some day (Philippians 2:10-11)?

In a world where friendships come and go, how does it make you feel to know that you have a constant friend in Jesus?

This passage speaks of the *kenosis,* or the "self-emptying" of Christ. It means that Jesus emptied himself of His prerogatives of deity. He did not cease being God. He voluntarily laid aside the use of His prerogatives as God. Now read John 1:1-14 again. The best description of the incarnation is found in verse 14: *"And the Word became flesh and dwelt among us, and we have seen his glory, glory as of the only Son from the Father, full of grace and truth."*

The story of the birth of Jesus Christ, the actual event of God becoming flesh, is recorded by Matthew and Luke. Matthew makes it clear that Jesus was born of a virgin. His birth was completely miraculous.

31. How did Mary conceive (Matthew 1:18-24)?

The Old Testament prophet, Isaiah, foretold this event 700 years before it happened: *"Therefore the Lord himself will give you a sign. Behold, the virgin shall conceive and bear a son, and shall call his name Immanuel* (Isaiah 7:14). Luke records Gabriel's announcement to Mary, and gives more details of the incarnation:

And behold, you will conceive in your womb and bear a son, and you shall call his name Jesus. He will be great and will be called the Son of the Most High. And the Lord God will give to him the throne of his father David, and he will reign over the house of Jacob forever, and of his kingdom there will be no end.

And Mary said to the angel, "How will this be, since I am a virgin?"

And the angel answered her, "The Holy Spirit will come upon you, and the power of the Most High will overshadow you; therefore the child to be born will be called holy—the Son of God." (Luke 1:31-35)

32. Luke also records that the angels announced the birth of Christ to shepherds (2:8-20). How do they identify the baby (2:11)?

Jesus promised that He would come again (John 14:3), and He referred to His return a number of times (Matthew 24:27, 30, 37, 39, 42, 44; 25:31).

33. Why did Jesus go back to heaven (John 14:1-2)?

34. Why will Jesus return (John 14:3)?

35. Why do you think the angels announced that Jesus would return (Acts 1:11)?

Peter proclaimed the return of Jesus as part of the gospel message (Acts 3:17-21).

36. What is one of the reasons Jesus will return (Acts 3:21)?

Moses (Deuteronomy 18:15) and all the prophets predicted the coming of one who would turn everyone from their wicked ways (Acts 3:22-26). When you read the entire context of Acts 3:17-21, it is clear who Peter believed that Moses was speaking of in Deuteronomy 18:15. He was the same one the prophets spoke of, the offspring of Abraham who would bless all peoples on earth, the one that God raised up from the dead, and the one who will wipe out the sins of the people and turn them from their wicked ways. Peter was specific. This one was the Christ (Messiah) and Lord. Peter even calls Him by name (Acts 3:20).

37. Peter believed Moses was speaking about____________.

Paul wrote about the return of Jesus (Philippians 3:20-21; 2 Thessalonians 1:7, 10; Titus 2:13), and he referred to it many times. He clearly tells the Thessalonians that the resurrection of the righteous dead will accompany the return of Christ.

For this we declare to you by a word from the Lord, that we who are alive, who are left until the coming of the Lord, will not precede those who have fallen asleep. For the Lord himself will descend from heaven with a cry of command, with the voice of an archangel, and with the sound of the trumpet of God. And the dead in Christ will rise first. Then we who are alive, who are left, will be caught up together with them in the clouds to meet the Lord in the air, and so we will always be with the Lord. Therefore encourage one another with these words. (1 Thessalonians 4:15-18)

The resurrection and return of Christ have several other implications for believers to consider. Paul tells the Corinthians that, at the last trumpet, the dead will be raised imperishable and the living will be changed instantaneously (1 Corinthians 15:51-52). The Bible also teaches that the unrighteous will be resurrected (Daniel 12:2; John 5:28- 29; Acts 24:15). The idea of the Second Coming includes a great final judgment for the unrighteous at some time in the future (Matthew 25:46; Mark 9:43-48; Revelation 19:20; 20:11-15; 21:8).

38. Memory Verses

Therefore he had to be made like his brothers in every respect, so that he might become a merciful and faithful high priest in the service of God, to make propitiation for the sins of the people. (Hebrews 2:17)

Have this mind among yourselves, which is yours in Christ Jesus, who, though he was in the form of God, did not count equality with God a thing to be grasped, but emptied himself, by taking the form of a servant being born in the likeness of men. And being found in human form, he humbled himself by becoming obedient to the point of death, even death on a cross. Therefore God has highly exalted him and bestowed on him the name that is above every name, so that at the name of Jesus every knee should bow, in heaven and on earth and under the earth, and every tongue confess that Jesus Christ is Lord, to the glory of God the Father. (Philippians 2:5-11)

39. Action Steps

Reread Hebrews 2:1-18. Record any observations you make. Especially look for references to the incarnation, Christ's humanity, and reasons for the incarnation, or the extent of the incarnation. For instance, Hebrews 1 points out that Christ is superior to the angels. What does it mean that God *"made him for a little while lower than the angels"* in Hebrews 2:6 and 2:9? This phrase refers to Jesus during His life on earth. Notice that He is *"now crowned with glory and honor because he suffered death."* It was from an exalted position that Jesus was temporarily made lower than the angels. Also, notice that there is a new dimension of joy and triumph at the accomplishment of God's plan of salvation.

40. Rethink the Lesson

- Think about some of the titles of Jesus.

- Jesus made certain claims that could only be made by God.

- Jesus was clearly aware of His divinity.

- Jesus forgives sins.

- Jesus created all things.

- Jesus is the very nature of deity.

- The purpose of the incarnation was that Jesus might be a faithful high priest, that He might make atonement for the sins of the people, and that He could give help to those who are being tempted.

- Jesus was made, for a time, a little lower than the angels that He might enter the human race. Now He stands highly exalted, with a name above all names, full of joy and triumph. He has completed God's plan of eternal redemption.

- Moses and the prophets told about the coming of Jesus.

- Jesus will return to take the righteous to heaven and judge the unrighteous.

Answers to Lesson 3

1. Lord

2. King of Israel

3. Faithful and True; Word of God; King of Kings and Lord of Lords

4. Christ, Son of the Living God; Messiah

5. Alpha and Omega, First and Last, Beginning and End

6. Root and Offspring of David; Bright and Morning Star

7. Your answer

8. Your answer

9. Your answer

10. They were amazed and said, *"Who is this who even forgives sins?"*

11. They said, *"Only God can forgive sins."*

12. Not one of them was sinless except Jesus.

13. Jesus was without sin.

14. Jesus is the Son.

15. God made the universe through the Son.

16. He is the image of the invisible God.

17. By his powerful word

18. Purification for sins

19. To seek and to save that which was lost

20. Give His life a ransom

21. To become a merciful and faithful high priest in service to God

22. That He might make atonement for the sins of the people

23. To help those who are being tempted

24. Nature of God

25. God

26. A servant

27. Human likeness, the appearance of a man

28. God highly exalted Jesus.

29. Above every name

30. Bow and confess that Jesus Christ is Lord

31. By the Holy Spirit

32. A Savior, Christ the Lord

33. To prepare a place for His disciples

34. To take His disciples with Him so that they might be with Jesus

35. Your answer

36. To restore everything

37. Jesus

Tahir's Story

"I just don't feel like I'm doing enough for God," said Tahir to John. It had been about three weeks since he had given his life to Christ.

"I hear you, Tahir. Many people struggle with that same feeling. But do you remember what we read in God's Word the other day? We don't have to do good works to earn God's approval."

"Yeah, I remember that."

John continued, "I understand that this is a big shift for you. You grew up following a works-based religion where you constantly had to earn Allah's favor with prayers, fasting, going to the mosque, and all that. But your new life in Christ is different."

Tahir leaned in with a look on his face that beckoned John to continue.

"There is nothing more to do to earn God's favor. Jesus took care of that on the cross. All of our sins, past, present, and future, were placed on Him that day. And because of that, we stand before God completely whole and justified."

Tahir sat back in his chair, pondering John's words. After a brief pause in the conversation, Tahir again leaned forward and replied, "You've told me this before. Why do I keep forgetting this truth, John?"

"It's a hard truth to grasp, Tahir. It's natural to want to work for our salvation, to try to pay off our sins by our own spiritual performance. Most every religion in the world outside of Christianity operates this way, but the Bible clearly states that we are saved by grace. And because Jesus died for our sins, we have assurance that we will be with Him in heaven one day!"

Lesson 4
Your New Path
Part One

Therefore, if anyone is in Christ, he is a new creation.
The old has passed away; behold, the new
has come. (2 Corinthians 5:17)

The Apostle Paul states, *"None is righteous, no, not one"* (Romans 3:10). Humankind's sinful nature has been passed on to all people because of Adam's sin. Everyone is born with this sinful nature and eventually acquiesces to sin, thereby giving approval to that sinful nature. Look at Genesis 3 and Romans 5:12.

1. How did sin enter the world?

2. What causes death?

3. Who sinned?

Jesus taught that sin comes from the heart (Matthew 15:18-19). Before people sin outwardly, they defile themselves with their own evil thoughts and intentions. Sin is more than committing wrong deeds. It is willful disobedience that comes from a sinful nature. Sin separates people from God, causing spiritual death, and eventually results in physical death. Adam and Eve were expelled from the Garden of Eden and from the presence of God. Read Romans 1:18-2:16. Sin erodes the image of God in people.

> What has been the most rewarding aspect of your new life in Christ?

Paul teaches that sin results in death (Romans 6:21). But under the law of righteousness, you have been set free from sin. As a slave to God, you reap holiness and eternal life (Romans 6:22). Salvation and righteousness in God's sight cannot be earned by attempting to do good deeds. God offered it to you freely as you believed on His Son. Romans 6:23 declares, *"For the wages of sin is death, but the free gift of God is eternal life in Christ Jesus our Lord."*

4. What are the wages of sin?

5. What is the gift of God?

6. Through whom can one receive that gift?

You may ask, "Does this free gift from God keep me from sinning?" The regenerating power and sanctifying power of the Holy Spirit puts away the old sinful nature. You are a new creation! As you grow and mature in Christ, you will learn more about what pleases God. But no one is perfect, and no one will reach perfection until he or she goes to heaven and is changed to be like Christ. You may still struggle with some issues or yield to temptation. You will study about spiritual warfare in Lesson 10. For now, be encouraged that God grants help in the face of temptation.

Read 1 Corinthians 10:1-13. Can you list four encouraging truths from verse 13?

7.

8.

9.

10.

Read James 4:7. What two suggestions does James make?

11.

12.

13. What does James say that the devil will do?

Now read 1 Peter 5:8-9. Satan wants to destroy you and your faith in Christ. Peter gives advice and encouragement.

14. His advice is …

15. His encouragement is …

The writer to the Hebrews tells us that Jesus gives help.

For because he himself has suffered when tempted, he is able to help those who are being tempted. (Hebrews 2:18)

Let us then with confidence draw near to the throne of grace, that we may receive mercy and find grace to help in time of need. (Hebrews 4:16)

If we say we have no sin, we deceive ourselves, and the truth is not in us. If we confess our sins, he is faithful and just to forgive us our sins and to cleanse us from all unrighteousness. (1 John 1:8-9)

16. What should we do if we sin?

17. What will God do?

Christians believe that sin has separated all humans from God. Each individual possesses culpability and can do nothing to reinstate that fellowship on his or her own initiative. All people deserve eternal punishment and banishment from the presence of God. Salvation refers to that act of God whereby He provides deliverance from the bondage, guilt, and penalty of sin. God provided salvation by offering Jesus as a sacrifice for the sins of the world. Ransom means to purchase something back that once belonged to the purchaser. Adam and Eve lived in fellowship with God, but sin broke that fellowship.

18. Why did Jesus come in human form (Matthew 20:28)?

For there is one God, and there is one mediator between God and men, the man Christ Jesus, who gave himself as a ransom for all, which is the testimony given at the proper time. (1 Timothy 2: 5-6)

Redemption is a term that means to free someone from something bad by paying a penalty. In the Old Testament, the sin offering had to be perfect, without blemish, or defect. John called Jesus the *"Lamb of God, who takes away the sin of the world"* (John 1:29, 36). Silver and gold could never pay the price to redeem sinful mankind. God redeemed us with the precious blood of Christ.

19. How does Peter describe Christ as the perfect sacrifice (1 Peter 1:18-21)?

John refers to Jesus as the Righteous One (1 John 2:1). That is why John could say, *"He is the propitiation for our sins, and not for ours only but also for the sins of the whole world"* (1 John 2:2). Because of the substitutionary death of His holy Son, a righteous God can pardon a guilty race without compromise. You may ask, "But how does an individual appropriate salvation?"

The Holy Spirit convicts people of their sin, convinces them concerning the righteousness of Christ, and convinces them of the reality of judgment (John 16:8-11).

What must the sinner do to be saved? Read Romans 10:9-11.

20. Paul said that in order to be saved, the sinner must confess with his mouth that _______________________.

21. And the sinner must believe in his heart that_______________________.

The whole sin problem begins with unbelief. The path to salvation begins with believing. It is not a matter of works and deeds. It is a matter of faith. We can call Romans 10:9-11 the Christian confession of faith. Of course, this is found in different forms in different places in the New Testament. Peter first made this confession by saying, *"You are the Christ, the Son of the living God"* (Matthew 16:16). In confessing Jesus as Lord, we are affirming to the church and to the world that we will serve and obey Jesus. By saying that we believe in the resurrection, we are also saying that we believe in His atoning death. The resurrection affirms the deity of Jesus: *"and was declared to be the Son of God in power according to the Spirit of holiness by his resurrection from the dead, Jesus Christ our Lord"* (Romans 1:4). Furthermore, the resurrection affirms the efficacy of His atoning death: *"Who was delivered up for our trespasses and raised for our justification"* (Romans 4:25). Peter told the crowd in Jerusalem that they must repent and be baptized (Acts 2:36-39). This means the sinner confesses and forsakes sin. The Holy Spirit changes the new believer by creating new life (John 3:3-8). God forgives sin and cancels the guilt and punishment (Romans 3:21-26; 8:1).

Now read Acts 13:38-39.

22. Paul proclaimed the forgiveness of sins through _______________.

23. Through Jesus everyone who believes is _______________.

Justification is a legal term. Believers are declared innocent, and God views them as though they never sinned. What a wonderful salvation Jesus provides for believers! How can a person be made righteous? Paul explains:

But now the righteousness of God has been manifested apart from the law, although the Law and the Prophets bear witness to it—the righteousness of God through faith in Jesus Christ for all who believe. For there is no distinction: for all have sinned and fall short of the glory of God, and are justified by his grace as a gift, through the redemption that is in Christ Jesus, whom God put forward as a propitiation by his blood, to be received by faith. This was to show God's righteousness, because in his divine forbearance he had passed over former sins. It was to show his righteousness at the present time, so that he might be just and the justifier of the one who has faith in Jesus. (Romans 3:21-26)

God's salvation provides so much for the believer. In your own words, what do the following verses say that <u>God's salvation provides</u> through Christ's sacrifice?

24. Acts 2:29-33

25. Acts 2:38-39

26. Romans 8:1

27. Romans 8:2

28. John 14:1-4

29. Hebrews 9:15

30. What do you think the eternal inheritance is in Hebrews 9:15?

31. John 10:27-28

32. John 3:1-3

These are just a few of the wonderful promises in God's Word for those who have put their faith in Jesus. We have forgiveness of sin, freedom from bondage, power to resist the devil, freedom from guilt and condemnation, God's presence living in us in the person of the Holy Spirit, assurance of eternal joy in the presence of God, and more.

33. Memory Verses

The thief comes only to steal and kill and destroy. I came that they may have life and have it abundantly. (John 10:10)

I have been crucified with Christ. It is no longer I who live, but Christ who lives in me. And the life I now live in the flesh I live by faith in the Son of God, who loved me and gave himself for me. (Galatians 2:20)

What then shall we say to these things? If God is for us, who can be against us? He who did not spare his own Son but gave him up for us all, how will he not also with him graciously give us all things? (Romans 8:31-32)

34. Action Steps

Take time to reflect on how great a salvation has been provided for you. Think about all of the provisions of God's grace. Now, thank Him and praise Him for not being a vindictive and capricious god. He is merciful and kind, not willing that any should perish. He has provided the right path for you. He wants to fellowship with you, help you to live victoriously, and take you to heaven to spend eternity with him. Hallelujah!

35. Rethink the Lesson

- All people sin because they have a sinful nature. They are guilty before God, and they can do nothing to pay for their sin.

- God gives us help to resist Satan and overcome temptation.

- God saved us by sacrificing His Son. The blood of Jesus redeemed humanity.

- The sinner must confess with his mouth that Jesus is Lord, and believe in his heart that God raised Jesus from the dead.

- Sinners must repent of their sins. Of course, this means that they must be sorry for their sinful nature, but it also means that they must be sorry for their unbelief, and change their minds about who Christ is. They must believe.

- The new believer receives many benefits of salvation.

Answers to Lesson 4

1. Through one man
2. Sin
3. All
4. Death
5. Eternal Life
6. In Christ Jesus our Lord

7. No temptation has seized you except what is common to man.

8. God is faithful.

9. He will not let you be tempted beyond what you can bear.

10. When you are tempted, God will provide a way for you to endure it.

11. Submit to God.

12. Resist the devil.

13. He will flee from you.

14. Resist him; stand firm in the flesh

15. You know that your brothers throughout the world are suffering the same things.

16. Confess our sins.

17. Forgive us our sins and cleanse us from all unrighteousness

18. To serve and give His life a ransom for many.

19. The precious blood of Christ, a lamb without blemish or defect

20. Jesus is Lord.

21. God raised Him from the dead.

22. Jesus

23. Is freed from everything from which you could not be freed by the law of Moses

24. The promised Holy Spirit

25. Forgiveness of sins and the gift of the Holy Spirit

26. No condemnation. This means no guilty conscience and freedom from culpability.

27. Freedom from the law of sin.

28. A destiny in heaven with Jesus

29. Eternal inheritance; eternal life in heaven; the presence of God; the blessings of God.

30. Your answer

31. Eternal life and security

32. The kingdom of God

Tahir's Story

"What you feed will live, and what you starve will die," said John to the young believer. Tahir had only been a Christian for a few weeks, and John was sharing about living in the Spirit versus living according to the flesh. "You must feed your spirit man and not give in to the ways of the flesh," he explained.

Tahir listened intently with his Bible and notebook in hand.

"But here's the good news," continued John. "Your desires have changed. You don't want to engage in the sins that you used to because of God's grace in your life. And, if you do stumble, you feel bad about it because you don't like those old ways. That's the conviction of the Holy Spirit, and His desire is to always draw you closer to himself. The devil condemns; The Holy Spirit convicts."

"Well, how do I live by the Spirit?" Tahir inquired.

John thought for a moment and replied, "By doing what you've been doing for the last four weeks." John had been discipling Tahir since the day this former Muslim gave his heart to Jesus.

They met regularly to discuss the Scriptures and apply them to daily life. The young believer felt that John was not only sharing the gospel with him, but his very life as well. They spent countless hours together, and Tahir was able to see how John's Christian faith informed every part of his life.

Lesson 5
Your New Path
Part Two

*I have been crucified with Christ. It is no longer I who live,
but Christ who lives in me. And the life I now live in the
flesh I live by faith in the Son of God, who loved me
and gave himself for me.* (Galatians 2:20)

Your new life is that of a disciple. A disciple is a follower. As a follower of Jesus Christ, we must model our lives after Him. He is our pattern and great example in all things. The disciple makes Christ the Lord of his or her life. A key verse for discipleship is in the Gospel of Luke: *"And he said to all, 'If anyone would come after me, let him deny himself and take up his cross daily and follow me'"* (Luke 9:23). Jesus gives three mandates to His disciples: (1) deny themselves, (2) take up their crosses daily, and (3) follow Christ.

The first characteristic of a disciple is self-denial. This means that you no longer live for your own goals, motives, and ambitions. Neither do you live for the wishes of your family or community. You are no longer self-centered in your life style; you are Christ-centered. You now live for Jesus.

The second characteristic of a disciple is self-discipline. *Cross-bearing* means redemptive ministry. The servant serves his or her Lord, and he or she serves others. The disciplined life focuses on the Bible, prayer, fellowship, and ministry. Notice the first two emphasize the disciple's relationship with the Lord, and the last two disciplines emphasize others, that is, believers and nonbelievers. We have already discussed the need for disciples to develop a regular practice of Bible reading and study. The last half of this lesson will deal with the discipline of prayer. The need for fellowship and ministry within the context of community is addressed in Lessons 8 and 9. These disciplines are all part of following your new path.

Have you encountered difficulties along this new path? How is God helping you through them?

The third characteristic of a disciple is following Christ, which includes obedience and fruit-bearing (Galatians 5:22-23). Fruit-bearing takes time, requires work on the disciple's part, and grows naturally as a result of remaining in Christ.

Read John 15:1-17.

1. How does one bear much fruit? (John 15:5)

2. How does remaining in Christ affect our prayer lives? (John 15:7)

3. **Bearing much fruit glorifies_______________ (John 15:8).**

4. **Bearing much fruit shows_______________ (John 15:8).**

Remaining in Christ, or remaining in His love, produces fruit in the disciple's life.

5. **How do we remain in Christ and in His love? (John 15:9-10)**

Now read Galatians 5:16-26.

6. **How do we overcome the desires of the sinful nature? (Galatians 5:16)**

Paul says that the sinful nature and the Spirit are in conflict with one another.

7. **What is the result? (Galatians 5:17)**

8. **But if you are led by the Spirit, you are not_________ (Galatians 5:18).**

The acts of the sinful nature are obvious (Galatians 5:19), and those who live according to them will not inherit the kingdom of God (5:21). However, disciples should live in the Spirit, and they will exhibit the fruit of the Spirit (5:22-23). Paul says there is no law against these (5:23). What does he mean? You will find the answer as you read 1 Timothy 1:9.

9. **Jesus is more emphatic in Luke 14:25-27 than in Luke 9:23. What does He say about someone who is unwilling to forsake all, carry his or her cross, and follow Jesus?**

Discipleship, that is, denying self, cross-bearing, and following Christ, will cost the disciple his or her life. Life changes radically. Death to self may not always be a figure of speech. Many followers of Christ have been martyred for their new lives. Look at Luke 9:23 in its context: Luke 9:21-27.

List three things the Son of Man must face (Luke 9:22).

10.

11.

12.

13. **Is it possible for a disciple's life to go on unchanged (Luke 9:23-24)?**

14. **What will happen if there is no change (Luke 9:24)?**

Holding on to the old life will kill spiritual life. The disciple will not grow spiritually, and he or she will die spiritually. Lifeless Christians do not produce fruit, do not contribute to ministry, do not contribute to the community life of the church, are poor witnesses of Christ, and they are in danger of reverting to their old life-style or religion.

15. What happens to the person who loses his or her life for Christ?

The phrase "whoever loses his life for me" is found in all four Gospels and in two Gospels more than once. No other saying of Jesus is given such emphasis. The culture of the kingdom of God is different than the world's culture. The standards, motives, goals, and life-styles of the followers of Christ are counter-culture to the world. Standing up against the world's ways is not popular, but Jesus promises that disciples will find new life in following Him. The life Jesus gives is full of joy, purpose, and satisfaction.

Some of those who were listening to Christ that day witnessed the coming of the kingdom of God (Luke 9:27). It was not ushered in militarily, but by the death of Christ upon His cross. Crosses are made to die upon, not carry. Jesus wants His disciples to deny themselves, pick up their crosses, follow Him, and die. What Christ meant is that a disciple must die to self and former life-styles and be willing to die literally, if necessary.

Sometimes dying to self involves losing our families. Christ's words in Luke 9:23-27 are found in Matthew 10:32-39 in a slightly different form. Matthew includes something else about the death of following Christ:

Do not think that I have come to bring peace to the earth. I have not come to bring peace, but a sword. For I have come to set a man against his father, and a daughter against her mother, and a daughter-in-law against her mother-in-law. And a person's enemies will be those of his own household. Whoever loves father or mother more than me is not worthy of me, and whoever loves son or daughter more than me is not worthy of me. And whoever does not take his cross and follow me is not worthy of me. Whoever finds his life

will lose it, and whoever loses his life for my sake will find it.
(Matthew 10: 34-39)

For many, the cost of following Christ may include losing family, community, financial security, identity, and significance as a person. They are in need of a new family and a new community. As previously mentioned, Lesson 8 will discuss the disciple's need to find his or her new family and community within the context of the church.

16. "Whoever finds his life will lose it" (Matthew 10:39). What does Jesus mean?

17. How does the phrase "and whoever loses his life for my sake will find it" give hope to the disciple who has been cut off from family and community (Matthew 10:39)?

Prayer is one of the disciplines of cross-bearing. When speaking of prayer, we are not talking about prescribed rituals, dry routines, vain repetitions, or meaningless forms.

We are talking about conversing with the Almighty. God hears our prayers, and He speaks to us. Old Testament life and theology placed heavy emphasis on prayer. John taught His disciples to pray (Luke 11:1). Jesus set an example before His disciples as He prayed regularly. One day His disciples came to him while He was praying. They did not ask Him to teach them how to preach powerfully, how to evangelize persuasively, how to interpret Scripture exactly, nor did they ask for enhancement of any other ministerial gift. Luke 11:1 says that one of His disciples said to Him, *"Lord, teach us to pray."* This was certainly an appropriate request because Jesus prayed often, emphasizing the importance of prayer by deed. Jesus prayed at His baptism (Luke 3:21), alone with His disciples (Luke.9:18), in certain places (Luke11:1), in the morning (Mark 1:35), withdrawn into solitude (Luke 5:16), all night on the mountainside (Luke 6:12), and before important events such as in the garden before His crucifixion (Luke 22:41). In the garden, He prayed in agony, earnestly, and according to His Father's will (Luke 22:41-44). Jesus prayed for Peter (Luke 22:32), for children (Matthew 19:13), for the coming of the Holy Ghost (John 14:16), for the elect (John 17:9), and He prayed for us to be kept from the evil in the world (John 17:15).

Now read Luke 11:2-13.

18. We are not praying to an impersonal deity, but to our___________.

19. His name is ___________________________. This means that His name is holy.

We should not attempt to impose our will upon the Almighty but invite His sovereignty to control our lives (Luke 11:2). Yet, we have the right to petition God for our daily needs (v. 3), especially our spiritual needs like repentance, grace to forgive, and deliverance from temptation (v. 4). Pray with persistence (vs. 5-10). Our heavenly Father is good; He gives us what we need, that is, the Holy Spirit who helps in all aspects of our lives (vs. 11-13).

Jesus said that His house was to be called a house of prayer (Matthew 21:13). The disciples learned their lesson well, and the New Testament church was a praying church: *"All these with one accord were devoting themselves to prayer,"* and *"And they were all filled with the Holy Spirit"* (Acts 1:14; 2:1-4). They prayed for the Lord's will at church business meetings (Acts 1:24). They devoted themselves to prayer (Acts 2:42).

20. What happened when the church prayed (Acts 4:31)?

The apostles gave themselves continually to prayer and the ministry of the word (Acts 6:4). They prayed when they set apart the deacons for ministry (Acts 6:6).

21. What happened when Peter and John prayed for the disciples in Samaria (Acts 8:17)?

22. What happened when Peter prayed for Dorcas (Acts 9:40)?

Peter prayed on a rooftop in Joppa. Cornelius prayed always, and his prayers were heard. The church prayed for Peter while he was in prison. They gathered and prayed in houses. The church in Antioch prayed, and they launched the church's first missionary endeavor (Acts 13:1-3). Paul and Barnabas prayed as they appointed elders in every church. Paul and Silas went outside the city of Philippi, expecting to find a place of prayer (Acts 16:13). Paul and Silas prayed in the Philippian jail (Acts 16:25).

Read the moving account as Paul bids farewell to the Ephesian elders (Acts 20:17-38).

23. What did they do (Acts 20:36-38)?

Before leaving the coast of Tyre, Paul knelt on the beach with the disciples of that area, along with their wives and children, and prayed (Acts 21:5). Peter commanded Simon to pray for forgiveness in Samaria (Acts 8:22).

24. What did James say to do if anyone is in trouble (James 5:13)?

25. What did he say to do if there is any sick among you (James 5:14-15)?

To the Romans, Ephesians, Philippians, Colossians, Thessalonians, and to Philemon, Paul said that he always prayed for them. The Spirit helps us in our prayer, and He prays through us (Romans 8:26-27).

Read 1 Corinthians 14:13-15.

26. Like Paul, we should pray with _________________ and with _________________.

27. How did Paul instruct the Ephesians to pray (Ephesians 6:18)?

28. Why should you pray for your pastor, for missionaries, and for others in ministry (2 Corinthians 1:11; Colossians 4:3)?

Actually, we are to pray for all saints (Ephesians 6:18) and to let our requests be known to God (Philippians 4:16). We are to pray continually (1 Thessalonians 5:17). Paul requests, *"Finally, brothers, pray for us, that the word of the Lord may speed ahead and be honored, as happened among you"* (2 Thessalonians 3:1). Jesus commanded His followers to pray for workers to be sent into the harvest field (Luke 10:2). Paul said, *"First of all, then, I urge that supplications, prayers, intercessions, and thanksgivings be made for all people, for kings and all who are in high positions, that we may lead a peaceful and quiet life, godly and dignified in every way"* (1 Timothy 2:1-2). James tells us to pray for one another

(James 5:16); Jude tells us to pray in the Holy Spirit (Jude 1:20). Jesus instructed us to even pray for those who persecute us (Matthew 5:44). He said to pray believing, in secret, and without vain repetitions (Matthew 6:5-8). In looking for the return of Jesus, we should watch and pray (Mark 13:33, KJV). If we ask the Lord for wisdom, He will give it (James 1:5).

29. How should we ask for wisdom (James 1:5-8)?

30. How can we avoid falling into temptation (Matthew 26:41)?

Pray always and do not lose heart; pray without pride, but as one pleading for mercy. Jesus said that some pray lengthy prayers for show, taking advantage of people, even widows. The angel told Cornelius that his prayers came up for a memorial before God, and Peter said that the Lord's ears are open to the prayers of the righteous (1 Peter 3:12). In Revelation 5:8, the prayers of the saints, as incense and as a vial of odors, rise to the throne of God. It is no wonder that Paul told Timothy, *"I desire then that in every place the men should pray, lifting holy hands without anger or quarreling"* (1 Timothy 2:8). If you ever come to the point where you do not know what to pray for, just refer to the previous list, and you will find plenty to pray about.

31. Memory Verses

And he said to all, "If anyone would come after me, let him deny himself and take up his cross daily and follow me." (Luke 9:23)

I am the vine; you are the branches. Whoever abides in me and I in him, he it is that bears much fruit, for apart from me you can do nothing." (John 15:5)

Pray then like this: "Our Father in heaven, hallowed be your name. Your kingdom come, your will be done, on earth as it is in heaven. Give us this day our daily bread, and forgive us our debts,
as we also have forgiven our debtors. And lead us not into temptation, but deliver us from evil." (Matthew 6:9-13)

32. Action Steps

If you do not practice a regular time of personal prayer, begin now! Do not wait another day! Set aside a time each day to be alone with God. Begin by using the study in this lesson. Read Scripture as you pray. Some portions of Scripture provide prayers for you. Make a prayer journal. List your requests as they come to mind. As you read over your list in prayer each day, cross off the ones that the Lord has answered. Pray to the Father in Jesus' name, and do not forget to give thanks.

33. Rethink the Lesson

- The three characteristics of discipleship are self-denial, self-discipline, and following Christ.

- The disciplined life focuses on Bible study, prayer, fellowship, and ministry.

- Remaining in Christ, or remaining in His love, produces fruit in the disciple's life.

- Obedience to Christ keeps us in His love.

- Jesus was our example. If He needed to pray, we need to even more.

- When the Early Church prayed, the Holy Spirit moved mightily.

- We should pray for our pastors and for all those in ministry.

- James said that we should pray in faith, believing that we will receive.

- Jude said that we should pray in the Holy Spirit. Lesson 9 will expand on that topic.

Answers to Lesson 5

1. Living in Christ and having Christ live in me

2. My prayer life will be powerful and effective.

3. The Father

4. Discipleship

5. Obey Christ's commands; this means obeying His words, or obeying the Word of God, the Bible.

6. Live by the Spirit

7. You will not gratify the desires of the sinful nature.

8. Under law

9. That person cannot be Christ's disciple.

10. Suffer many things.

11. Be rejected by the elders, chief priests, and teachers of the law.

12. Be killed, and on the third day be raised to life.

13. No

14. The spiritual life will die.

15. That disciple will have a fulfilled life, eternal life, and a life full of God's blessings.

16. Whoever values life more than following Christ will not inherit eternal life.

17. God will replace the hurt of losing family and loved ones with the joy of His presence.

18. Father

19. Hallowed

20. The place was shaken; all were filled with the Holy Spirit, and spoke the word of God boldly.

21. They received the Holy Spirit.

22. She opened her eyes and sat up.

23. They knelt down together, prayed, wept, embraced, and kissed.

24. Pray

25. Call for the elders of the church to pray over him and anoint him with oil in the name of the Lord

26. With my spirit and with my mind (understanding).

27. Pray in the Spirit.

28. Prayer helps those in ministry. Also, prayer opens doors of ministry.

29. Believe and do not doubt.

30. Watch and pray.

Tahir's Story

"Tahir, you're always smiling," said one of the young believer's classmates at school. "Why are you so happy?"

"Well, Jesus died for my sins and rose again to bring me close to the Father," began Tahir. "And He put the Holy Spirit within me to comfort me and give me peace every day. So, I guess I'm happy because I'm in constant communion with the Creator of the Universe. It's pretty cool."

At that, the classmate walked away shaking his head in disbelief.

"*Perhaps I came on too strong*," Tahir thought. But someone else was listening.

Ricky approached Tahir. "You're a Muslim, right?"

"I was, Ricky, for all my life until about two months ago."

"I thought I noticed something different about you lately."

"Yes, it's been amazing!" Tahir was always glad to share about what Jesus had done in his life.

"Well," continued Ricky, "I didn't mean to be listening in on your conversation, but I've just got to ask a question.

"Sure!"

"I know about Jesus and God and all that, but what's the Holy Spirit?"

"The Holy Spirit is God, Ricky! He is the third Person of the Trinity. When Jesus ascended into Heaven after God the Father resurrected Him, He promised that He would send a Helper to be with His disciples. And, I'm telling you, it is awesome to know that God is with you and even in you!"

"So do you feel the Holy Spirit?" asked Ricky.

"I feel Him leading and guiding me. I feel Him directing my steps and showing me what to say, like when I'm praying for someone or just having a casual chat like this. Yes, I definitely feel Him."

Ricky was intrigued. "So, how does somebody get to know God the way you do?"

At this, the two walked together to the school cafeteria and continued their conversation. Tahir was thankful for these Holy Spirit-led moments.

Lesson 6
Your New Helper
Part One

And I will ask the Father, and He will give you another Helper, that He may be with you forever.
(John 14:16, NASB).

Who is the Holy Spirit? The Bible uses various names to refer to the Holy Spirit. Each designation emphasizes a unique task or aspect of the Spirit's character.

- The Holy Spirit (Luke 11:13; Romans 1:4)

- The Spirit of grace (Hebrews 10:29)

- The Spirit of truth (John 14:17; 15:26; 16:13; 1 John 5:6)

Which of these descriptions of the Holy Spirit is most important to you?

- The Spirit of life (Romans 8:2)

- The Spirit of Wisdom and Knowledge (Isaiah 11:2)

- The Spirit of glory (1 Peter 4:14)

- The Spirit of God and of Christ (1 Corinthians 3:16; Romans 8:9)

- The Holy Spirit of promise (Ephesians 1:13, NASB)

The Bible portrays the Holy Spirit as a person, as God, as God's gift, as one who will be with you forever, and as your Helper.

Notice how Jesus referred to the Holy Spirit as a person.

1. John 14:16-17

2. John 14:26

The Bible assigns personal characteristics and duties to the Holy Spirit. Note how the following verses suggest that the Holy Spirit is a person:

3. Romans 8:26-27; 15:30

4. 1 Corinthians 12:11

5. John 16:8-14

6. Acts 13:2; 16:6

Note how people treat the Holy Spirit like a person.

7. Acts 5:3

8. Isaiah 63:10

9. Ephesians 4:30

10. Acts 7:51

Has the
Holy Spirit
surprised you
along this
new
journey?

11. Hebrews 10:29

The Bible teaches that the Holy Spirit is divine. Christians believe that He is the third person of the Trinity and that He is coequal with the Father and the Son.

12. Who does the Apostle Peter suggest that the Holy Spirit is (Acts 5:3-4)?

The church as a body of believers (1 Corinthians 3:16-17), and the physical bodies of individual believers (6:19-20) are sacred because the Holy Spirit lives in them collectively and individually.

13. To whom is the Holy Spirit linked in these verses?

In the second lesson, we learned that there are certain qualities that describe God. The same qualities are given to the Holy Spirit:

14. 1 Corinthians 2:10-11

15. Luke 1:35

16. Romans 15:19

The Holy Spirit does things that only God does.

17. Genesis 1:2; Job 33:4; Psalm 104:30

18. John 3:5-8; Titus 3:5

19. Romans 8:11

20. 2 Timothy 3:16; 2 Peter 1:21

Notice how the Holy Spirit is associated with the Father and the Son in such a way that shows equality (Matthew 28:19; 2 Corinthians 13:14; 1 Peter 1:2).

In addition to the works of the Spirit already mentioned in proof of His personality and divinity, the Holy Spirit empowered certain individuals for particular tasks in the Old Testament. The Spirit gave Bezalel special abilities in craftsmanship for the construction of the tabernacle (Exodus 31:3-5), gave Joseph gifts of administration (Genesis 41:38), and empowered the judges with charismatic leadership (Judges 3:10; 6:34). The Spirit anointed prophets, priests, and kings for special service.

Jesus is the best example of someone empowered by the Spirit. Jesus is Isaiah's "Servant of the Lord" in chapter 42. He will bring justice to the nations, be a covenant for the people and a light for the Gentiles, open blind eyes, free captives from prison, and release those who sit in darkness from the dungeon (Isaiah 42:1-9). Verse 10 bursts into a song of jubilation for the salvation that is brought to the ends of the earth.

21. How does the Servant of the Lord accomplish all of this (Isaiah 42:1)?

The Spirit of the Lord GOD is upon me, because the Lord has anointed me to bring good news to the poor; he has sent me to bind up the brokenhearted, to proclaim liberty to the captives, and the opening of the prison to those who are bound; to proclaim the year of the LORD's favor, and the day of vengeance of our God; to comfort all who mourn; to grant to those who mourn in Zion—to give them a beautiful headdress instead of ashes, the oil of gladness instead of mourning, the garment of praise instead of a faint spirit; that they may be called oaks of righteousness, the planting of the LORD, that he may be glorified. (Isaiah 61:1-3)

22. To whom is Isaiah referring?

The Spirit descended upon Jesus at His baptism (Matthew 3:16; Mark 1:10; Luke 3:22; John 1:33). The Spirit then led Jesus into the wilderness to be tempted by the devil for forty days

(Matthew 4:1). Scripture implies that the Spirit controlled Jesus. In case there was any doubt, Luke says that Jesus was *"full of the Holy Spirit ... and was led by the Spirit into the wilderness"* (Luke 4:1).

23. How was Jesus led? (Luke 4:1)

24. How did Jesus return to Galilee after His forty days of temptation (Luke 4.14)?

Read Luke 4:14-21. Jesus applied Isaiah's words (Isaiah 61:1-3) to himself. Once Luke established that Jesus ministered in the power of the Holy Spirit, we can assume that He continued in the Spirit.

Notice the impact of the Spirit upon Jesus in the following passages.

25. Luke 4:28-30

26. Luke 4:31-32

27. Luke 4:33-37

28. Luke 4:38-40

The same Holy Spirit who empowered Jesus Christ is available to help believers today. Jesus said that He would not leave us alone, but He would send another "Helper" (John 14:16, NASB), and He promised that the Helper would be with us forever. Jesus then identifies the Helper as the Holy Spirit (John 14:26).

In the following passages, identify ways in which the Holy Spirit helps believers.

29. John 3:3-6

How has the Holy Spirit helped you in your daily life?

30. 2 Corinthians 3:18 (This refers to the Spirit's help in the process of sanctification.)

31. 1 Peter 1:2

32. Galatians 5:16

33. Galatians 5:22-26

34. Romans 8:13

35. John 14:25-26

36. John 15:26-27

37. John 16:13-14

38. How long will the Spirit remain with Jesus' disciples (John 14:16)?

39. Memory Verses

But the Helper, the Holy Spirit, whom the Father will send in my name, He will teach you all things, and will bring to your remembrance all that I said to you. (John 14:26, NASB)

The grace of the Lord Jesus Christ and the love of God and the fellowship of the Holy Spirit be with you all. (2 Corinthians 13:14)

Jesus answered, "Truly, truly, I say to you, unless one is born of water and the Spirit, he cannot enter the kingdom of God." (John 3:5)

40. Action Steps

Read John 14, 15, and 16. List the things that the Holy Spirit does for believers. What is the Spirit's chief ministry to unbelievers?

41. Rethink the Lesson

- The Holy Spirit is a person. He possesses characteristics of personality, performs personal acts, and He is treated like a person.

- The Holy Spirit is God.

- The Holy Spirit empowered certain individuals in the Old Testament for special tasks.

- Jesus was anointed by the Holy Spirit. His work was done completely by the power of the Spirit. Jesus is our great example and model. If Jesus depended upon the help of the Holy Spirit, how much more do we as human beings need the Spirit's help in our lives?

- The Holy Spirit helps disciples by regenerating, sanctifying, empowering, teaching, guiding, and illuminating the truth about Jesus.

Answers to Lesson 6

1. He, the Holy Spirit, lives with you and will be in you.

2. He teaches.

3. He helps, intercedes, and loves.

4. He gives gifts.

5. He convicts.

6. He sets apart for ministry, calls into ministry, and He leads and directs in ministry.

7. People may lie to the Spirit.

8. People may grieve the Spirit.

9. People may grieve the Spirit.

10. People may resist the Spirit.

11. People may outrage the Spirit.

12. God.

13. God

14. The Holy Spirit is all-knowing.

15. The Holy Spirit is all-powerful.

16. The Holy Spirit is all-powerful.

17. He creates.

18. He regenerates or gives new life to the believer.

19. He has resurrection power.

20. He inspired the writers of Scripture.

21. God put His Spirit on Him.

22. The Messiah. He was referring to Jesus.

23. Jesus was led by the Spirit.

24. He returned in the power of the Spirit.

25. He received divine protection and provision to escape danger.

26. He taught with authority.

27. He had authority over evil spirits.

28. He healed the sick and cast out demons.

29. He gives new life and initiates people into the kingdom of God.

30. He transforms you into the likeness of Christ.

31. He sanctifies you.

32. He helps you to overcome the desires of the sinful flesh.

33. The Spirit guides you (NRSV).

34. The Spirit helps you to put to death the deeds of the body, and you will live.

35. He will teach you all things.

36. He will witness of Jesus and help His disciples (you) to do so also.

37. He guides disciples into all truth. He speaks of things to come by giving the apostles the spirit of prophecy so they could tell about the future and end times. He glorifies Christ by making Him known.

38. Forever

Tahir's Story

"What was that?" Tahir asked John. Tahir had just gone to the altar to give his life to Christ. He started worshipping God after praying with the youth pastor. With hands raised, he was thanking Jesus for the amazing gift of salvation. Then, to his surprise, strange words started coming from his lips. It appeared to be a language unfamiliar to him.

"That's the baptism in the Holy Spirit," replied John joyfully. "You are speaking in tongues!"

Tahir looked puzzled. Later, John would explain everything. For now, however, he wanted his friend to enjoy God's presence. "Keep it up! Just let the Holy Spirit do a work in you."

Later that day, John walked Tahir through the Book of Acts, showing him that when the Holy Spirit came upon believers, they received the initial physical sign of speaking in tongues. He also shared concerning how the Holy Spirit empowers believers to be witnesses of the Good News of Jesus. This excited Tahir to no end, as he was eager to share his newfound faith with anyone who would listen.

"What a day this has been!" exclaimed John. "You gave your life to Christ *and* now you've been baptized in the Holy Spirit!"

Lesson 7
Your New Helper
Part Two

But you will receive power when the Holy Spirit has come
upon you, and you will be my witnesses in Jerusalem
and in all Judea and Samaria, and to
the end of the earth. (Acts 1:8)

In the same way that the Spirit helped Jesus in ministry, He helped the apostles and believers in the Early Church to fulfill the church's mission. John identified Jesus as the Christ, the Lamb of God who takes away the sin of the world, the Son of God, the one who would carry out judgment, and the one who would baptize with the Holy Spirit (Mark 1:7-8; Luke 3:15-17; John 1:29-34). Jesus told His disciples that the gospel would be preached in His name to all nations, that He would send His Father's promise, and that the Father would empower them (Luke 24:47-49). Luke links the promised gift of the Father with empowerment, the baptism of Holy Spirit, and the Great Commission (Acts 1:4-8).

On the Day of Pentecost, the Holy Spirit filled all of the disciples, and they began to speak in other tongues (Acts 2:4). Pentecost fulfilled Joel's prophecy (Joel 2:28-29; Acts 2:16-21). Peter remembered the words of Jesus: *"For John baptized with water, but you will be baptized with the Holy Spirit not many days from now"* (Acts 1:5). Then he explained:

This Jesus God raised up, and of that we all are witnesses. Being therefore exalted at the right hand of God, and having received from the Father the promise of the Holy Spirit, he has poured out this that you yourselves are seeing and hearing. (Acts 2:32-33)

For Peter, Pentecost affirmed the resurrection, ascension to heaven, and lordship of Jesus (Acts 2:34-36). When the people heard, they wanted to know what to do (Acts 2:37):

And Peter said to them, "Repent and be baptized every one of you in the name of Jesus Christ for the forgiveness of your sins, and you will receive the gift of the Holy Spirit. For the promise is for you and for your children and for all who are far off, everyone whom the Lord our God calls to himself." (Acts 2:38-39)

The promised Holy Spirit is available to everyone who believes and repents of their sinful nature. When a person repents and believes, that individual is born of the Spirit (John 3:3-8). If you have repented and believe that Jesus is the Son of God, that He died for your sins, and that God has raised Jesus from the dead, then the Holy Spirit lives in you! We call this regeneration. The Holy Spirit has created new life in you.

Have you experienced the Holy Spirit's power emboldening you to be a witness?

What happened at Pentecost supplied the disciples with power for giving witness to the gospel. Jesus had returned to the Father and was baptizing believers in the Holy Spirit. As the Spirit had empowered

Old Testament saints for special ministries, and as the Spirit had empowered Jesus Christ for ministry, now the Spirit would make a difference in the lives of the apostles and believers in the Early Church. Pentecostals believe that the Spirit's work in regeneration and the baptism in the Holy Spirit are two separate experiences of the Spirit for the believer. They may, at times, seem to occur simultaneously (Acts 10:44-46), and, at other times, there may be a time interval between the experiences (Acts 19:1-7). It is more important to notice that there is a distinctive difference in the purpose of the two separate experiences. Regeneration creates new life in the believer. He or she becomes alive to the Spirit, and God lives in the believer by the Spirit. The believer begins to grow in his or her new life. The baptism in the Holy Spirit supplies the new believer with power for service. Do you think the baptism in the Holy Spirit made a difference in the lives of the early believers?

1. **Compare Luke 22:54-62 with Acts 2:38-41. Explain the difference that the baptism in the Holy Spirit made in the Apostle Peter.**

We have seen that Jesus ministered by the power of the Spirit of God, and His authority was given to Him by the anointing of the Holy Spirit. The apostles ministered in Jesus' name, or by the authority given to them by Jesus. Jesus baptized the early believers in the Holy Spirit, empowering them as He promised (Acts 1:4-8).

2. **Make your own observations on Acts 3:1-16**

Jesus mentioned that the Holy Spirit would help us know what to say when speaking for Him (Matthew 10:17-20; John 14:26; 16:12-14).

3. **How did Peter give such powerful witness (Acts 4:5-13)?**

4. What effect did the infilling of the Spirit have upon the early believers (Acts 4:31)?

Read Acts 5:17-42.

The power and joy that the Holy Spirit supplied in the lives of the believers in Jerusalem could not be silenced by persecution or threats. Perhaps you have been persecuted or threatened for your faith in Jesus Christ. You need the power of the Holy Spirit to help you. Take particular note of Acts 5:41: *"Then they left the presence of the council, rejoicing that they were counted worthy to suffer dishonor for the name."*

Now, read Acts 7:1-59.

5. How could Stephen preach with such power, face death with such courage, and forgive his persecutors? (See Acts 6:5; 7:55)

Missionaries have documented the necessity of the baptism in the Holy Spirit for converts from Islam. Converts often face persecution, isolation, and physical danger. Those who have not received God's power through the baptism in the Holy Spirit more often revert to Islam because of extreme pressure. The Spirit helps people just as He helped believers in the book of Acts.

Persecution broke out against the church in Jerusalem (Acts 8:1). The believers, except for the apostles, were scattered throughout Judea and Samaria. Philip preached the word in a certain city in Samaria, and many believed and were baptized. The apostles in Jerusalem sent Peter and John to them, and when they arrived, they prayed for them to receive the Holy Spirit. By this time, the apostles felt that it was necessary for all believers to receive the same experience that they received on the Day of Pentecost.

Describe the events of the following passages:

6. **Acts 2:1-4**

7. **Acts 10:44-46; 11:15-16**

8. **Acts 19:1-7**

9. **What occurred in all three instances where people were baptized in the Holy Spirit?**

In Acts 8:15-17, Peter and John prayed and laid hands on the disciples in Samaria, and they received the Holy Spirit. There is no mention that they spoke in tongues, but something visible did occur. It was so demonstrative that Simon attempted to purchase the ability to dispense the Holy Spirit. The passage does not describe what that was, but from the other three instances it seems obvious.

Have you been baptized in the Holy Spirit with the initial physical evidence of speaking in tongues?

10. **What do you think happened in Samaria?**

Acts 9:1-19 gives an account of Saul's conversion and baptism. Acts 13:9 indicates that Saul was also called Paul. Although Scripture does not explicitly state that Paul spoke in tongues when he was filled with the Spirit, we have reason to believe that he did.

11. Note what Paul said to the Corinthians (1 Corinthians 14:18):

The baptism in the Holy Spirit empowers believers for ministry. In Lesson 9, you will learn about gifts the Spirit has to help you in your ministry. In Lesson 10, you will learn about spiritual weapons to do battle against the enemy of your soul.

12. Memory Verses

And it shall come to pass afterward, that I will pour out my Spirit on all flesh; your sons and your daughters shall prophesy, your old men shall dream dreams, and your young men shall see visions. Even on the male and female servants in those days I will pour out my Spirit. (Joel 2:28-29)

But you will receive power when the Holy Spirit has come upon you, and you will be my witnesses in Jerusalem and in all Judea and Samaria, and to the end of the earth. (Acts 1:8)

When the day of Pentecost arrived, they were all together in one place. And suddenly there came from heaven a sound like a mighty rushing wind, and it filled the entire house where they were sitting. And divided tongues as of fire appeared to them and rested on each one of them. And they were all filled with the Holy Spirit and began to speak in other tongues as the Spirit gave them utterance. (Acts 2:1-4)

13. Action Step

Every believer needs to be baptized in the Holy Spirit. You need your new Helper. You have seen what the Helper did for Jesus, the apostles, and the early believers. He still helps believers today, and He wants to fill you and help you in your Christian life. Remember, the baptism in the Holy Spirit is the gift of God. You can ask for this gift because you are a follower of Jesus Christ. Receive it by faith. As you pray and ask Jesus to baptize you in the Holy Spirit, just begin to worship, praise God, and exalt Jesus Christ. When the Holy Spirit fills you, you will begin to speak and praise God in an unknown language. Do not be afraid of this phenomenon. Neither should you be so concerned with speaking in tongues that you seek the experience of tongues. Seek the baptizer, Jesus Christ. Just allow waves of praise and joy to fill you and overflow. You will be filled with inexpressible joy, and you will begin to experience power in your life that you need in order to be an effective witness for Jesus Christ. If you have already experienced the baptism in the Holy Spirit, now would be an appropriate time to thank God and allow him to bless you again with His holy presence.

How has your life changed since you were filled with the Holy Spirit?

14. Rethink the Lesson

- The Holy Spirit supplies power for believers to complete the church's mission.

- In Lesson 5, we noted that the baptism in the Holy Spirit was predicted by the Old Testament prophet Joel, by John the Baptist, and by Jesus himself.

- The baptism in the Holy Spirit is separate from salvation in function.

- The baptism in the Holy Spirit helped believers by giving them power and courage in the face of persecution and even martyrdom.

- The apostles felt that it was important that every believer be filled with the Holy Spirit.

- As believers are baptized in the Holy Spirit, they praise God in unlearned languages.

Answers to Lesson 7

1. Your answer

2. When we minister in Jesus' name, we minister under His authority. He gave the Holy Spirit to empower disciples. Ministering in the authority of Jesus is ministering with the anointing of the Holy Spirit.

3. Verse 8 says that He was filled with the Holy Spirit.

4. They spoke the word of God boldly where before they were timid.

5. Stephen was full of the Holy Spirit.

6. All were filled with the Holy Spirit and began to speak in tongues.

7. The Holy Spirit came on all who heard the message. Peter and the circumcised knew that the Holy Spirit had come upon them because they heard the Gentiles speaking in tongues—just as the Spirit had come on them in the beginning.

8. After these disciples were baptized in water, Paul laid his hands on them. The Spirit came on them, and they spoke in tongues and prophesied.

9. They all spoke in tongues when the Spirit came upon them.

10. Your answer

11. Paul thanked God that he spoke in tongues more than all of the Corinthians.

Tahir's Story

"Tahir, we're here for you," said the pastor. "Whatever you need, you let us know."

Tahir was overwhelmed with how his life had changed in the two months since becoming a believer in Jesus. Not only did he have a relationship with God, something he had been seeking his whole life, but he also had a new family—the church. In addition to John, other believers spent time with Tahir and even called him if he missed a church service. He felt like he was home.

Because of his newfound faith, Tahir's family disowned him. The support and encouragement of his brothers and sisters in Christ was essential.

Lesson 8
Your New Community
Part One

*...the household of God, which is the church of the
living God, a pillar and buttress of the truth.*
(1 Timothy 3:15)

The New Testament gives instructions for disciples on living in community and in the world. For Christians, living in community means relating to other believers as members of the church. The Church includes all born-again believers who have been placed into the body of Christ by the Spirit of God (1 Corinthians 12:13). The term *church* is used to refer to individual groups of believers (Galatians 1:2; Colossians 4:15-16), and to the universal Church (Ephesians 1:22-23; Colossians 1:18).

Jesus said to Peter, *"I will build my church, and the gates of hell shall not prevail against it"* (Matthew 16:18). In the Great Commission, Jesus told the eleven to *"make disciples of all nations*" (Matthew 28:19). He did not mention church planting in the Great Commission. However, the apostles knew that their task would be to evangelize, make disciples out of the converts, and group these converts into communities of believers called churches. Thus, the primary ministry of the apostles was making disciples and planting churches. Although Jesus initiated His Church, the apostles, especially Paul, through the power of the Holy Spirit, articulated what the Church should be. Paul uses metaphors to describe the church and to describe the disciples who make up the church.

Read Ephesians 2:19-22. Before knowing Jesus, you were a foreigner and an alien to God's Kingdom.

1. As a disciple of Christ, how does Ephesians 2:19 describe you?

The emphasis is on community. You are not just a citizen, but a fellow citizen with God's people. Citizenship indicates rights and obligations. As part of the church there are certain blessings and responsibilities. As you participate in a local church, you will be ministered to, but you should also mature to the point where you are making a contribution to the overall ministry of the church. Some Christians have never learned that they have a responsibility to minister to others.

2. What other metaphor does Paul use (Ephesisans 2:19)?

He uses this more than once in his letters to refer to the church. The word *household* has often been referred to as immediate family or extended family. However, in God's family there are no cousins; all are sons and daughters, brothers and sisters. Family membership suggests greater intimacy and greater responsibility than citizenship does. Family members love and care for one another. In the household, babies are nurtured, children are educated and, at times, disciplined; mature adults assume responsibilities for the welfare of the family, and care for the sick and elderly. This is all done in an atmosphere of love and acceptance. The idea of membership indicates equal partnership, and membership has rights. Joy and sorrow are shared. Family members are helped, encouraged, and depended upon. Birth, baptism, graduation, marriage, raising a family, and death sometimes all take place within the context of one local congregation. Sometimes because of relocation, a disciple has the privilege of being part of two or more local church families in his or her lifetime. Experiences, both sad and joyous, are shared. Religious holidays are shared experiences within the context of the church.

In Ephesians 2:20, Paul's metaphorical language switches to that of a building.

3. The foundation refers to the founding work and the teachings of whom (Ephesians 2:20)?

The redemptive work of Christ established the church. He said, *"I will build my church"* (Matthew 16:18). He is the chief cornerstone (Ephesians 2:20). The terminology, *"joined together"* (Ephesians 2:21), shows close relationship exists between members and between Christ and the members. Disciples are building material; Peter says, living stones (1 Peter 2:4).

4. How does God live in such a temple (Ephesians 2:22)?

Paul's favorite metaphor of the church is the "body of Christ." Christ ministered through His physical body on earth; now His body is the church. In the ancient world, it was common imagery to speak of individuals who were part of a larger group and drawn together for a common purpose as members and the group as a body.

We need to note several things about this image. First, it shows the church's unity and diversity. Members, although many and diverse, are interdependent as they perform Christ's work (1 Corinthians 12:12). Second, it depicts the universal Church (Ephesians 1:20-23) and individual local bodies (1 Corinthians 12:27). Third, the image of the body of Christ shows us the relationship of the church as a group of believers with Christ.

5. Christ is the ______________________________(Colossians 1:18).

6. How did Christ provide peace (Colossians 1:19-20)?

Finally, the image of the body of Christ demonstrates relationships as they should be between individuals in the church. Christians never live individually in relationship to the Lord without regard for others. Read 1 Corinthians 12:12-27. Paul develops the concept of interrelatedness and interdependence among the members of the body. The metaphor of the human body teaches us that the body is one complete unit only as all of its functioning members are healthy and in place. In the body of Christ, each member is an integral part of the whole. Members are formed into one body by their common experience in the Spirit.

7. According to 1 Corinthians 12:12-14, the body is one, but made up of ______________________________.

Each member has a unique function, and all members need one another (1 Corinthians 12:14-24).

8. Who has *"combined the members of the body"* (1 Corinthians 12:24)?

9. There should be no _________________________________ (1 Corinthians 12:25).

10. What should members have for each other, according to 1 Corinthians 12:25?

11. What do parts of the body share (1 Corinthians 12:26)?

12. What does the Bible say you are (1 Corinthians 12:27)?

The body of Christ is the most wonderful community when it is functioning properly. The body in Corinth was not functioning properly, and Paul wrote the letter to correct them. The New Testament continually instructs believers to demonstrate Christ's love. Jesus commanded His disciples to love one another (John 13:34).

13. What is the evidence of true discipleship (John 13:35)?

Paul explained how much disciples should love one another: *"Love one another with brotherly affection. Outdo one another in showing honor"* (Romans 12:10). Peter encouraged believers to *"love one another earnestly from a pure heart"* (1 Peter 1:22).

14. How did Paul characterize unbelievers in 2 Timothy 3:1-5?

Paul uses the metaphor of the temple to instruct the Corinthians concerning their common experience with the Spirit (1 Corinthians 3:16-17).

15. According to 1 Corinthians 3:16-17, where does the Holy Spirit live?

Paul addresses division in the church in Corinth. They are building God's temple in Corinth. The church is not to be destroyed by divisions, controversies, or other sins because it is the temple of the Holy Spirit. God will destroy anyone who does anything to damage the temple, the local church (1 Corinthians 3:17). This metaphor teaches disciples what their attitude should be toward the church, and how they should treat individual members and the body as a whole.

How has becoming a part of a Christian community helped you to grow in Christ?

The church exists to edify the saints and equip them for ministry. In this regard, the church's mission is to form Christ in each believer. Read Ephesians 4:7-13. Jesus himself gave gifts to the church: apostles, prophets, evangelists, pastors, and teachers.

16. What is their purpose in Ephesians 4:12?

17. Who is going to do the "works of service" or ministry (4:12)?

18. What is the ultimate goal (4:12)?

Notice the three-fold effect of having the body edified: (1) unity in faith and in the knowledge of the Son of God, (2) maturity, and (3) having Christ formed in us (4:13).

Now read the description of mature disciples (Ephesians 4:14-16).

Jesus intended the church to be the agency for evangelizing the world (Matthew 28:19-20). He placed the responsibility upon the church in three progressive stages. He first commissioned the Twelve: *"And he appointed twelve (whom he also named apostles) so that they might be with him and he might send them out to preach and have authority to cast out demons"* (Mark 3:14-15).

The second stage occurs when the Lord commissions the seventy-two (Luke 10:1-16). They are not only sent, but also told to pray that the Lord of the harvest would send even more laborers into the harvest (Luke 10:2). Luke emphasizes the divine nature of the commission of the Twelve and of the Seventy: *"The one who hears you hears me, and the one who rejects you rejects me, and the one who rejects me rejects him who sent me"* (Luke 10:16). Luke seems to restate John's account: *"As the Father has sent me, even so I am sending you"* (John 20:21).

Third, the Lord widened the scope of His mission to involve the entire church. It is likely that Jesus gave the Great Commission on several different occasions. However, the fact that the authors of Scripture recorded the Great Commission four times, and possibly five, if we count John 20:21, demonstrates the importance and urgency of the mission (Matthew 28:18-20; Mark 16:15-18; Luke 24:46-49; John 20:21; Acts 1:7-8). Evangelizing the world is the responsibility of every disciple. All believers should support missions and ministries of the church with their prayers and finances. Not all members will be pastors, evangelists, or missionaries, but every disciple should be involved in ministry of some kind, and every disciple should be attempting to bring family and friends to Jesus.

The account in Matthew emphasizes the making of disciples; this is discipleship. Mark's account emphasizes going and preaching to the whole world; this is world missions. Luke's account emphasizes the preaching of repentance and forgiveness of sins; this is evangelism. John's account emphasizes the sender; this is authority. In Acts, Luke's account emphasizes empowerment for witnessing.

The community of Christ's disciples live in the world among unbelievers. One of the responsibilities of all disciples is to live as witnesses in the world. God expected the Old Testament saints to be holy because they represented a holy God to the nations (Exodus 19:4-6; Leviticus 11:45). The Lord wanted His people to be free from the sins of surrounding nations, not contaminating themselves by taking wives from neighboring peoples (Ezra 9:1-10:44). The writers of the Old Testament constantly warned Israel concerning idolatry and protested false religion and evil culture while presenting high standards. The Ten Commandments (Exodus 20:1-17) declared unprecedented ideals, and the sacrificial system provided atonement for sin while teaching consecration to God and separation from the defilements of the world.

Like Old Testament believers, Christians represent a holy God. Not only does evangelism involve preaching a message, but it also includes presenting Christ-like character. The Apostle Paul desired to form Christ in the lives of his disciples (Galatians 4:19).

19. The believer's sanctification and righteousness is in __________ (1 Corinthians 1:30).

This has to do with the believer's position before God. However, Paul makes it clear that believers' lives should mirror their standing: *"Since we have these promises, beloved, let us cleanse ourselves from every defilement of body and spirit, bringing holiness to completion in the fear of God"* (2 Corinthians 7:1).

Read Galatians 5:16-26.

20. Paul says that disciples should walk by __________ (Galatians 5:16)

21. As disciples walk by the Spirit, they will not gratify the desires of the __________________________ (Galatians 5:16).

True disciples strive to exemplify Christ's holy character. Paul addresses issues such as Christian concern for one another (1 Corinthians 12:12-26; Ephesians 4:32), attitudes (Ephesians 4:29-31), and morality (1 Corinthians 5:1-5). He said that God wants disciples to avoid sexual immorality (1 Thessalonians 4:3-6). *"For God has not called us for impurity, but in holiness"* (1 Thessalonians 4:7). Disciples of Christ live differently.

> *Therefore be imitators of God, as beloved children. And walk in love, as Christ loved us and gave himself up for us, a fragrant offering and sacrifice to God. But sexual immorality and all impurity or covetousness must not even be named among you, as is proper among saints. Let there be no filthiness nor foolish talk nor crude joking, which are out of place, but instead let there be thanksgiving. For you may be sure of this, that everyone who is sexually immoral or impure, or who is covetous (that is, an idolater), has no inheritance in the kingdom of Christ and God. (Ephesians 5:1-5)*

22. List the qualities of holy people (Colossians 3:12-15, NIV).

Most of the Apostle Peter's first letter addresses issues of self-control and Christian conduct in relationships. He exhorts believers to holy living (1 Peter 1:13-2:12). They should conduct themselves accordingly because they live among unbelievers: *"Keep your conduct among the Gentiles honorable, so that when they speak against you as evildoers, they may see your good deeds and glorify God on the day of visitation"* (1 Peter 2:12).

Jesus said that His disciples should not limit their concern to Christians. Disciples of Christ love their enemies and pray for their persecutors; otherwise they are no better than the tax collectors and pagans (Matthew 5:43-47). This kind of love reflects God's selfless love and defies human logic. Human nature wants revenge against enemies. This is the way of the world, the way of Satan. Jesus wants His disciples to be different. Solomon stated the principle in the Old Testament: *"If your enemy is hungry, give him bread to eat, and if he is thirsty, give him water to drink"* (Proverbs 25:21). John the Baptist preached benevolence (Luke 3:11). Jesus said, *"Give to the one who begs from you, and do not refuse the one who would borrow from you"* (Matthew 5:42). Paul exhorted believers in Rome to help the needy and practice hospitality (Romans 12:13). Benevolence includes helping and doing good deeds.

23. Who should disciples help or do good to (Galatians 6:10)?

24. Who else should they do good to, according to Hebrews 13:16?

The mission of the church includes humanitarian work. The church relieves misery and suffering not because of legalistic duty, but because of Christian love.

25. Memory Verse

So then you are no longer strangers and aliens, but you are fellow citizens with the saints and members of the household of God. (Ephesians 2:19)

26. Action Steps

If you are not an active member of a Bible-believing church, begin looking for a Spirit-filled group of believers to participate in their worship and ministry. If you are already in fellowship or are a member of a church, talk to the pastor or an elder concerning ministry opportunities. Pray about what your gifts are and ask God to direct you into ministry.

27. Rethink the Lesson

- The New Testament uses the term *church* to refer to a local group of disciples, and to refer to the universal group of believers from all ages.

- Disciples are fellow citizens of God's Kingdom.

- Disciples are family members of the household of God.

- Disciples are building blocks in the temple of God, the habitation of the Spirit of God.

- The metaphor of the temple teaches disciples that they should love one another and treat one another with respect.

- The world will know the disciples of Christ by their love for one another.

- Evangelizing the world is the responsibility of every disciple.

- Every disciple should be involved in ministry, and every disciple should be attempting to bring family and friends to Jesus.

- Disciples of Christ display Christ's holy character by living by the Holy Spirit.

- True disciples display love not only for other disciples, but also for unbelievers.

Answers to Lesson 8

1. Fellow citizens with God's people and members of God's household

2. God's household or family

3. The apostles and prophets

4. By His Spirit

5. Christ is the head of the body.

6. Christ provided peace through His blood that was shed on the cross.

7. Members

8. God

9. Division in the body

10. Equal care for one another

11. Suffering and rejoicing

12. The body of Christ, and each one is a member of it

13. Fellow disciples love one another.

14. Lovers of self

15. In you, collectively, with all the disciples, and in you, individually.

16. To prepare God's people for ministry

17. The saints

18. Maturity

19. Christ

20. The Spirit

21. Sinful nature or flesh

22. Compassionate, kind, humble, gentle and patient, forgiving, loving, peaceful, and thankful. God's people should live in unity.

23. All people, especially to those who belong to the family of believers

24. Others

Tahir's Story

"Tahir, has God shown you what your spiritual gifts are?" inquired John. The two were doing a Bible study on this subject.

The young believer replied, "I'm not sure; I hadn't really thought about it."

"I'd like us to take some time to seek the Lord about your gifts. This will help you to discern the best area in which to serve at the church.

"Do you know what my gift or gifts might be?"

"I think so, but I don't want to tell you yet. I want you to pray about it, and we'll see if we come up with the same thing!" teased John.

Tahir smiled but was not amused. He wanted John to just tell him what his gift was, but that was not John's style. The mature believer continued, "Tahir, this is a really important subject. See, you don't just come to church to sit and listen to the singing, give in the offering, and hear a good sermon. You are a part of the body of Christ, and you have a purpose to fulfill here. That is why we're going to pray together that God would reveal to us what your gifts are. And, not too long from now, I'd like to see you serving in some capacity at the church."

"Wow," Tahir thought to himself. *"I could serve in the church?"* Just over two months ago he was attending Islamic clases, and now he may have the opportunity to serve in a Christian congregation! He was overjoyed at the thought.

Lesson 9
Your New Community
Part Two

*To him be glory in the church and in Christ Jesus
throughout all generations, forever and ever.
Amen.* (Ephesians 3:21)

An important part of living in community for disciples of Christ is corporate worship. The Old Testament gives the model as it describes public worship: *"Then Jehoshaphat bowed his head with his face to the ground, and all Judah and the inhabitants of Jerusalem fell down before the LORD, worshiping the LORD"* (2 Chronicles 20:18; cf. 1 Kings 8:62).

1. **What do you think Jehoshaphat is expressing by his posture and form of worship?**

The New Testament does not prescribe certain prayer postures or forms for worship. It seems that variety is encouraged. Nevertheless, at times, it is appropriate to bow down in reverence to an all-powerful, holy, and majestic God: *"And when he had said these things, he knelt down and prayed with them all"* (Acts 20:36). The Old Testament describes other forms of worship: *"The whole assembly worshiped, and the singers sang, and the trumpeters sounded. All this continued until the burnt offering was finished"* (2 Chronicles 29:28). Various Psalms repeatedly call the people to corporate worship:

> *Oh come, let us sing to the LORD; let us make a joyful noise to the rock of our salvation! Let us come into his presence with thanksgiving; let us make a joyful noise to him with songs of praise! For the LORD is a great God, and a great King above all gods. In his hand are the depths of the earth; the heights of the mountains are his also. The sea is his, for he made it, and his hands formed the dry land. Oh come, let us worship and bow down; let us kneel before the LORD, our Maker! For he is our God, and we are the people of his pasture, and the sheep of his hand. (Psalm 95:1-7)*

List six expressions of worship mentioned in Psalm 95:1-7.

2.

3.

4.

5.

6.

7.

List six reasons to worship God from Psalm 95:1-7.

8.

9.

10.

11.

12.

13.

In the New Testament, Jesus intended the church to worship the Father in Spirit, not emphasizing location, form, or posture (John 4:23). Paul gives instruction to the Corinthians concerning their conduct in worship and their obvious lack of concern for each individual (1 Corinthians 12-14). The context suggests that the problem manifested itself in public worship services, showing that the church modeled corporate worship after worship in the Old

Testament. The author of Hebrews emphasized the importance of gathering together (Hebrews 10:25). The author may have had in mind meeting together for fellowship, Bible study, partaking of communion, and prayer. These are all elements of the worship service. Prayer most certainly includes praise, adoration, and thanksgiving.

Christians believe that Christ instituted certain rites that serve as visible signs of God's saving grace. Many call these rites ordinances, since Christ ordered them to be observed. The ordinance of baptism by immersion is commanded in the Scripture. All who repent and believe on Christ as Savior and Lord are to be baptized. These disciples declare to the church and to the world that they have died with Christ and that they have also been raised with Him to walk in newness of life (Matthew 28:19; Mark 16:16; Acts 10:47-48; Romans 6:4).

Christians recognize Holy Communion, or the Lord's Supper, as a commemoration of Christ's suffering and death. Christians believe that Jesus established the Lord's Supper (Matthew 26:26-28; Mark 14:22-25; Luke 22:17-20; 1 Corinthians 11:23-27). Most recognize the necessity of repeating the ceremony regularly. The Lord's Supper symbolizes the fellowship that believers have with the Lord and with one another. The symbols express our sharing of the divine nature of our Lord Jesus Christ (2 Peter 1:4), memorialize His suffering and death, and prophesy His Second Coming (1 Corinthians 11:26).

The Holy Spirit gives gifts for the fellowship, life, and ministry of the church. The Apostle Paul explains that diversity, not uniformity, characterizes a healthy church, and he stresses the need for diversity within unity (1 Corinthians 12:4-31). It does not seem like Paul provides us with a complete or exhaustive list of spiritual gifts. Paul gives three lists of gifts (1 Corinthians 12:8-11, 12:28; 12:29-30). There is some overlapping in the lists. The lists should be understood as examples and callings of the Spirit. The list is merely representative of the diversity of the Spirit's mani-festations. Paul gives a considerable list so that the Corinthians will stop being so narrow-minded in their own emphasis.

In 1 Corinthians 13, Paul teaches believers to exercise gifts with love and concern for all members of the body. The individual who speaks in tongues speaks to God (1 Corinthians 14:2). His spirit is edified, but without interpretation the group receives no benefit. Since speaking in tongues accompanies the baptism in the Holy Spirit, believers in Corinth found it easy to exercise the gift of tongues by faith in the congregation, neglecting other gifts and thereby neglecting the needs of other members. The Spirit gives gifts for the edification of the entire church. When the Spirit edifies the body, He edifies each and every member. Likewise, as the Spirit ministers to members individually, the whole body is edified.

Spiritual gifts provide supernatural enablement for believers to minister not only to the body of Christ, but also to unbelievers. The Spirit's ministry to unbelievers mainly has to do with convincing and convicting. The Spirit will convict the world of sin, that is, unbelief, convince sinners of the righteousness that is only found in Jesus Christ, and convince the world of certain judgment (John 16:8-11).

But if all prophesy, and an unbeliever or outsider enters, he is convicted by all, he is called to account by all, the secrets of his heart are disclosed, and so, falling on his face, he will worship God and declare that God is really among you. (1 Corinthians 14:24-25)

One worker who has ministered among Muslims for many years testifies concerning the value of spiritual gifts for drawing unbelievers:

Preaching Christ in the Power of the Holy Spirit gets Muslims' attention and confirms Christ's claims. I know of Muslims who came to Christ because of the work of the gifts of the Spirit. Fadhila was attracted to the church because people there spoke in tongues! And even before she accepted the Lord in her life, she expressed her amazement at such a miracle and once she said to me: "To speak in a language that you never learned is really a witness that God is in you!" Today she is a strong believer and is baptized in the Holy Spirit.

14. What will people who minister in the gifts of the Spirit witness concerning Jesus Christ (1 Corinthians 12:3)?

There are different kinds of gifts and ministries but only one Lord and one God (1 Corinthians 12:4-6).

15. Who receives the manifestation (this means a spiritual gift) of the Spirit (1 Corinthians 12:7)?

16. Who is to benefit (1 Corinthians 12:7)?

17. Who determines who receives which gift (1 Corinthians 12:11)?

In a previous lesson we discussed the importance of every member of the body of Christ (1 Corinthians 12:12-26). In this context you can see that every member needs to be ministered to, and every member needs to be used by the Holy Spirit in ministry. Pray and ask the Spirit about which gift or gifts He wants to give you to minister to the body. Read 1 Corinthians 12:27-31. The questions in verses 29-30 are rhetorical. Not all people have any one particular gift and, conversely, we can deduce that no individual possesses all of the gifts.

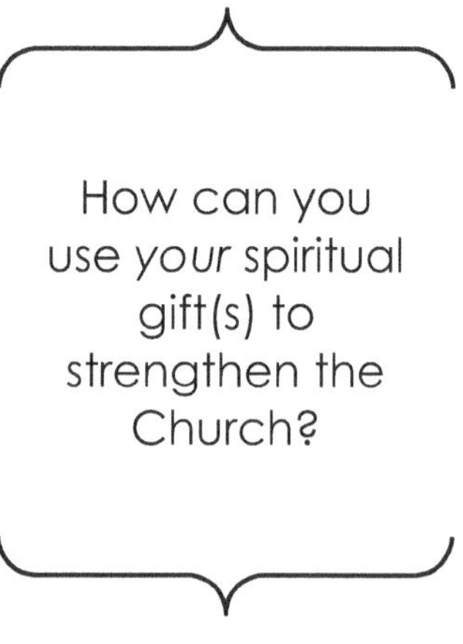

18. What does Paul say disciples should do (12:31)?

"Earnestly desire" includes praying and asking God to be used in spiritual gifts.

1 Corinthians Chapter 13 is not simply an interlude between chapters 12 and 14. This great chapter about love instructs disciples how the gifts are to be exercised. When they are used in love, they are used to benefit others. Disciples minister in the gifts out of compassion and concern for those who are in need.

1 Corinthians Chapter 14 begins with the same exhortation with which chapter 12 ended. Paul reemphasizes the need to desire and pray for spiritual gifts. Misuse of the gifts by some should not discourage others to desire to use the gifts correctly.

19. When one speaks in tongues, he or she speaks to ______________ (1 Corinthians 14:2)?

When disciples speak in tongues, they speak mysteries with their spirits (1 Corinthians 14:2), and in private worship, praying in tongues benefits them.

20. Speaking in tongues without interpretation edifies __________________ (1 Corinthians 14:4).

Notice three important things:

a. From the context, we conclude that no gift is greater than another gift. As all members are important, all gifts are needed. What then, are the "higher gifts" spoken of in 1 Corinthians 12:31? Most Pentecostal scholars agree that whatever gift is needed at the time is the greatest. Spiritual gifts are to meet the needs of the members of the body and the body as a whole.

b. 1 Corinthians 12 and 14 are not diminishing the importance of the gift of tongues. They are merely saying that in public worship, speaking with understanding, that is, prophecy, is better than tongues. If the gift of tongues is accompanied by the gift of interpretation, it is equally beneficial to prophecy for the body.

   c. The rhetorical question, *"Do all speak with tongues?"* (1 Corinthians 12:30) refers to the gift of speaking in tongues as used in the public worship service. All disciples should pray in tongues in private devotions. Paul said that he spoke in tongues more than all of the Corinthians (1 Corinthians 14:18). He also tells them that he wishes that they all spoke in tongues (1 Corinthians 4:5). It would be better that they prophesy in the public worship service unless there is interpretation, but this does not change the fact that disciples should pray in tongues regularly in private.

What are the nine gifts of the Spirit listed in 1 Corinthians 12:8-10?

21.

22.

23.

24.

25.

26.

27.

28.

29.

What gifts are listed in 1 Corinthians 12:28?

30.

31.

32.

33.

34.

35.

36.

37.

What gifts are listed in 1 Corinthians 12:29-30?

38.

39.

40.

41.

42.

43.

44.

45. Memory Verses

Oh come, let us worship and bow down; let us kneel before the LORD, our Maker! For he is our God, and we are the people of his pasture, and the sheep of his hand. (Psalm 95:6-7)

But the hour is coming, and is now here, when the true worshipers will worship the Father in spirit and truth, for the Father is seeking such people to worship him. God is spirit, and those who worship him must worship in spirit and truth. (John 4:23-24)

And I heard every creature in heaven and on earth and under the earth and in the sea, and all that is in them, saying, "To him who sits on the throne and to the Lamb be blessing and honor and glory and might forever and ever!" And the four living creatures said, "Amen!" and the elders fell down and worshiped. (Revelation 5:13-14)

46. Action Steps

As a disciple of Christ, you must obey Him and follow Him in water baptism. Your testimony will be loud and clear, "I am a disciple of Jesus Christ." If you have not been attending church, start to worship, fellowship, and minister in a local church. Join that body and support it with your attendance, prayer, fellowship, and finances. The church is supported only as believers pay tithes and give offerings. If you have not been receiving Communion, start participating. As the pastor explains the service, allow the rich meaning to bless, nourish, and encourage you. Let the symbolism remind you of the Lord's work and your participation as a member in the body of Christ. Finally, if you have not thought about the gifts of the Spirit for ministry, study Paul's letters and pray about what God wants to do through you and for you. By faith, receive the gift or gifts He has for you, and begin exercising those gifts so that you can fulfill your part as a member of the body of Christ.

47. Rethink the Lesson

- Form and posture are not as important as worshiping God freely in spirit and in truth.

- Disciples should participate in the ordinances of the church.

- Spiritual gifts provide supernatural enablement for disciples to minister to the body.

- Disciples should ask God to give them the gifts He wants them to have.

Answers to Lesson 9

1. Reverence, submission, your answer

2. Sing for joy.

3. Make a joyful noise.

4. Thanksgiving

5. Songs of praise

6. Bow down in worship

7. Kneel before the Lord our maker

8. He is the Rock of our salvation.

9. He is a great God.

10. He is the great King above gods.

11. He is the creator and sustainer of the universe (vs. 4-5).

12. He is our God.

13. He cares for us like a shepherd.

14. Jesus is Lord.

15. Each one

16. The common good; in other words, the body

17. The Spirit

18. Earnestly desire the greater gifts.

19. God

20. Himself/herself

21. Message of wisdom

22. Message of knowledge

23. Faith

24. Gifts of healing

25. Miraculous powers

26. Prophecy

27. Distinguishing between spirits

28. Speaking in different kinds of tongues

29. The interpretation of tongues

30. Apostles

31. Prophets

32. Teachers

33. Workers of miracles

34. Those having gifts of healing

35. Those able to help others

36. Those with gifts of administration

37. Those speaking in different kinds of tongues

38. Apostles

39. Prophets

40. Teachers

41. Working miracles

42. Gifts of healing

43. Speak in tongues

44. Interpret

Tahir's Story

"What's going on here?" Tahir thought, as he walked up the driveway to his front door. All of his belongings were piled on the front lawn.

Earlier that day, Tahir had been invited to distribute Christian tracts by a high school Bible study group. He decided to participate despite the fact that his sister also attended the school and she may find out about his newfound faith. Apparently, she did, he surmised, which caused his family to throw all of his belongings into the front yard.

"Either stop this Christianity nonsense or get out of my house," said Tahir's father, as his son slowly opened the front door. Tahir had no intention of walking away from Christ, but what was he going to do?

The young believer went to one of his father's stores and called the first person who came to his mind. "John," began Tahir, choking back tears, "I've been kicked out of my house."

A tone of concern carried John's response. "I am so sorry, Tahir. Where are you?"

Tahir told John the location of his father's store.

"Stay right there," John said. "I'm coming to pick you up. You've got a place to stay."

John's family took the bewildered believer in and eventually convinced Tahir's dad to let him come back home. The next six years, however, were very difficult for Tahir.

His father would not let Tahir attend church services, although he could go to the youth group. When he looked for his Bible, he would often find it in the trash or some other place where it shouldn't be. Indeed, quite early in Tahir's Christian walk he faced one of the greatest challenges of his life. Though he desperately wanted the approval of his family, especially his father, pleasing his Heavenly Father had become more important to him. Tahir kept praying and believing that one day his relationship with his earthly family would be reconciled. In the midst of these years of family hardship, he was careful to put on the full armor of God to stand against the endless onslaughts of the enemy.

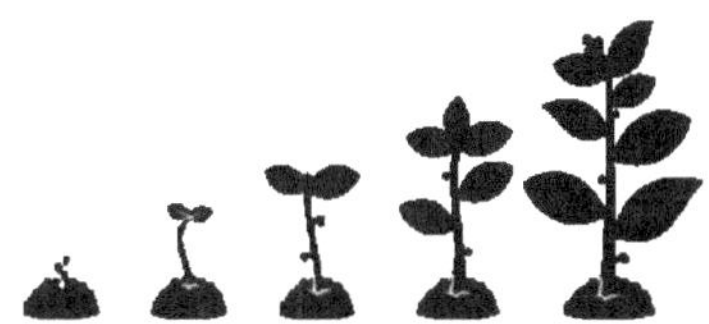

Lesson 10
Your New Struggle

For we do not wrestle against flesh and blood, but against the
rulers, against the authorities, against the cosmic powers
over this present darkness, against the spiritual forces
of evil in the heavenly places. (Ephesians 6:12)

The enemy was first introduced in Genesis 3 as a serpent. John identifies the great dragon as the serpent of Genesis 3, and if there were any doubts, he clearly identifies him as Satan, the devil (Revelation 12:9; 20:2). The devil persuaded Adam and Eve to doubt God, disobey his Word, and sin.

1. According to John, what does the devil do (Revelation 12:9)?

God pronounced enmity between the devil and humankind (Genesis 3:15). In typical fashion, the serpent strikes at the heel of a man, but a man crushes the head of the snake. In the history of spiritual warfare, Satan strikes, wounds, and does injury to humankind. Likewise, he wounded Jesus. However, Jesus struck the fatal blow to Satan. His final victory came by dying on the cross to rescue men and women from the clutches of sin (Colossians 2:14-15). God proclaimed a sentence upon Satan. Jesus won the victory, but it will only take an angel of God to cast him into the "Abyss" for a thousand years (Revelation 20:1-3). He will be released for a time to deceive the nations and wage war against God's people. Final judgment is executed as the devil is thrown into the lake of burning sulfur to be continually tormented forever (Revelation 20:1-10).

Christianity is not a system of this world. The world's religions are hostile toward the gospel of Jesus Christ. Whether they are steeped in law and hold their adherents in bondage to a worldly system, or whether they are full of demonic activity and keep their followers in bondage to dark powers, these religions are anti-Christ. Often, people who follow them do not live peacefully with followers of Jesus.

Millions of people live in fear of evil spirits, blaming their circumstances on external forces beyond their control. Some attribute the incidental inconveniences of everyday life to the spirits, while others blame demons for disease, famine, war, and death. They feel helpless and powerless without the help of someone, something, or some place that has perceived power to counteract the effect of evil forces. Multitudes of people turn to magic, witchcraft, and other ways of manipulating the spirit world. These folks are more concerned with the answers to the problems of everyday life than with the questions concerning God, eternity, and judgment.

The Holy Scripture assumes the reality of the spirit world and the operation of spirit beings in the earthly realm. The New Testament records that God's choice servant, Jesus, dealt with evil spirits more than once. On one occasion, He encountered an evil spirit in a house of prayer in Capernaum and ordered the spirit to come out of the man. The evil spirit shook the man violently and came out of him with a shriek. The people were amazed that He taught with such authority and that even the evil spirits obeyed Him (Mark 1:23-27).

Although Satan is a powerful being, and though humans are no match for him, Jesus' victory over the devil gives His disciples authority and power over the works of the devil now. Followers of Christ do not have to live under Satan's bondage or live in fear of his power. Disciples do not use superstition, witchcraft, or sorcery to engage the forces of the devil. Jesus said, *"The one who hears you hears me, and the one who rejects you rejects me, and the one who rejects me rejects him who sent me"* (Luke 10:16).

2. What did Jesus say that He gave to His disciples (Luke 10:19)?

3. What did Jesus give His disciples power or authority to do (Matthew 10:1)?

4. James said, if we *"resist the devil, he will*_________ (James 4:7).

Read Ephesians 6:10-18.

Scripture arms disciples with an arsenal of spiritual weapons to help them in their struggle against the enemy. Paul begins by encouraging the Ephesians to be strong in the Lord and His mighty power. By this he reminds disciples that they do not have to rely on their own resources to combat the forces of hell.

5. Whose strength and mighty power do we trust to protect us against evil (Ephesians 6:10)?

Paul reminds his disciples that there is spiritual armor to help them stand against the devil's attacks. And then he informs them that the struggle is not against flesh and blood. Our enemies are not people! God loves all people.

6. Identify the enemy (Ephesians 6:12).

A disciple needs the full armor of God (Ephesians 6:13). List the parts of the disciple's armor.

7. (6:14)

8. (6:14)

9. (6:15)

10. (6:16)

11. (6:17)

12. (6:17)

Some have identified truth as the Word of God (Ephesians 6:14). In the same context, Paul uses another metaphor to describe the Word of God (v. 17), and he leaves no room for misunderstanding. He states that the sword of the Spirit is the Word of God. So it seems unlikely that he would mix metaphors in the context while he is listing parts of the armor. While the Word is the source of truth, this is not the primary implication in Ephesians 6:14. It may include the idea of the Word or the Bible, but truth speaks of character and integrity. Disciples need integrity of character in order to stand. All spiritual weapons and gifts hang on one's character as all parts of a warrior's armor are buckled together by this belt. If the belt of truth is not buckled, no part of the armor will be available.

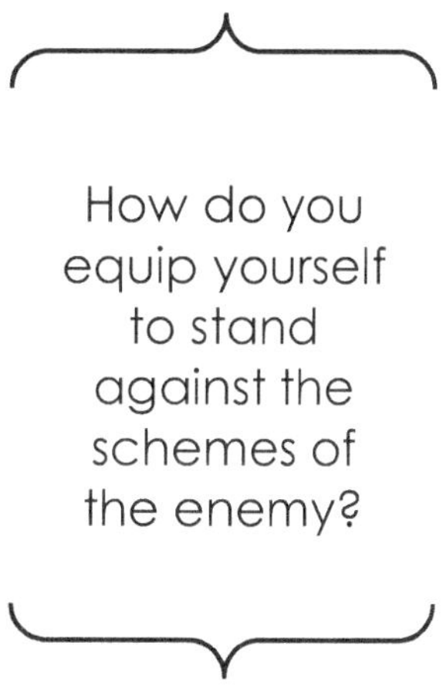

The "breastplate of righteousness" (Ephesians 6:14) primarily speaks of the righteousness of Christ. The devil cannot accuse disciples because Christ is the disciple's righteousness.

13. Who is the *"accuser of our brothers"* (Revelation 12:10)?

When God looks at the disciple, He does not see human weaknesses and sinful nature, but rather the righteousness of Christ. Although self-righteousness is as a polluted garment (Isaiah 64:6), the disciple's heart and conscience should be clear, and his or her life should reflect Christ's holy character. The breastplate of "righteousness" is to be in "place."

Although runners usually ran barefoot, the soldier required combat boots to support and protect his feet. Is it strange that Paul uses the metaphor of soldiers' combat boots to refer to the gospel of peace? No. Disciples struggle with the enemy in bringing the gospel of peace to a troubled world. Actually, these combat boots are referred to as *"the readiness given by the gospel of peace"* (Ephesians 6:15).

14. Comment as to what you think *"readiness"* means in this context.

The *"shield of faith"* will "extinguish all the flaming darts of the evil one" (Ephesians 6:16). The Roman soldier's shield was covered with leather and could be soaked in water, and it was capable of putting out flame tipped arrows. Satan will attempt to make disciples doubt, but these *"flaming darts"* are extinguished by nothing else but faith. Against all odds, Abraham believed God: *"Abraham believed God, and it was counted to him as righteousness"* (Romans 4:3).

Our faith is not detached from our intellect. Paul tells the Ephesians to take the *"helmet of salvation"* (Ephesians 6:17). The decision to follow Christ is a conscious decision and an act of volition or will.

I appeal to you therefore, brothers, by the mercies of God, to present your bodies as a living sacrifice, holy and acceptable to God, which is your spiritual worship. Do not be conformed to this world, but be transformed by the renewal of your mind, that by testing you may discern what is the will of God, what is good and acceptable and perfect. (Romans 12:1-2)

Furthermore, disciples need to guard what they allow to enter their minds. They need the helmet of salvation to protect their thought processes from destructive ideas. Disciples of Christ should be discreet as to what they view, read, or listen to. They have been saved and delivered from such deeds.

It has often been stated that the *"sword of the Spirit"* (Ephesians 6:17) is the only offensive weapon in the soldier's arsenal of armor. Nothing is more effective against the enemy than the Word of God and prayer. Disciples who neglect these disciplines in their lives are not effective in their struggle against evil. God wants Christians to be victorious, not defeated. That is why Paul uses the imperative when mentioning the armor of God.

After listing the spiritual armor, Paul gives some good advice. First, he urges the disciples in Ephesus to be *"praying at all times in the Spirit, with all prayer and supplication"* (Ephesians 6:18).

15. What does Paul mean when he says, "Praying, at all times, in the Spirit?"

Praying in tongues edifies one's own spirit (1 Corinthians 14:4). While this is not the goal of public worship, edifying ourselves strengthens us in our struggle against the enemy. Perhaps this is why Paul said, *"I thank God that I speak in tongues more than all of you"* (1 Corinthians 14:18). Disciples should pray every day. They should pray with the understanding, but for greater spiritual power, they should also pray in the Spirit. Paul told the Ephesians that when they pray in the Spirit they should pray all kinds of prayers and make requests. This is one reason why it is important to be baptized in the Holy Spirit. You may not be used by the Spirit in the gift of tongues in the public worship service, but every disciple can become a spiritual giant, a warrior in the struggle against the forces of evil. Pray in the Spirit every day. Jude echoes Paul's advice: *"But you, beloved, building yourselves up in your most holy faith and praying in the Holy Spirit, keep yourselves in the love of God, waiting for the mercy of our Lord Jesus Christ that leads to eternal life"* (Jude 1:20-21).

When we pray in the Spirit, we pray without the understanding (1 Corinthians 14:14). Paul told the Romans that there are times when we do not know what we ought to pray for, but the Spirit intercedes for us (Romans 8:26). This is why disciples need to pray in the Spirit in order to succeed in their struggle against the forces of evil.

16. How frequently should disciples pray (Ephesians 6:18)?

Many Christians, including Pentecostals, believe that the atonement provides healing for our physical bodies: *"Surely he has borne our griefs and carried our sorrows; yet we esteemed him stricken, smitten by God, and afflicted. But he was pierced for our transgressions; he was crushed for our iniquities; upon him was the chastisement that brought us peace, and with his wounds we are healed"* (Isaiah. 53:4-5). Read Matthew 8:16-17.

17. How did the writers of the New Testament interpret Isaiah 53:4-5?

18. What should we do if someone is sick (James 5:14-16)?

19. Memory Verses

For we do not wrestle against flesh and blood, but against the rulers, against the authorities, against the cosmic powers over this present darkness, against the spiritual forces of evil in the heavenly places. (Ephesians 6:12)

But you, beloved, building yourselves up in your most holy faith and praying in the Holy Spirit, keep yourselves in the love of God, waiting for the mercy of our Lord Jesus Christ that leads to eternal life. (Jude 1:20-21)

For the weapons of our warfare are not of the flesh but have divine power to destroy strongholds. We destroy arguments and every lofty opinion raised against the knowledge of God, and take every thought captive to obey Christ. (2 Corinthians 10:4-5)

20. Action Steps

Read Ephesians 6:10-18 every day this week. Memorize the parts of the disciple's armor. Think of ways to *"put on the whole armor of God."* Practice it. If you have been baptized in the Holy Spirit, pray in the Spirit every day this week. If you have not been filled with the Spirit with the evidence of speaking in tongues, then continue to ask the Lord to baptize you. As a disciple of Jesus, you need the infilling of the Holy Spirit in your new struggle.

21. Rethink the Lesson

- The devil is the disciple's enemy.

- The systems of this world are anti-Christ.

- Jesus has given His disciples authority and power over Satan and the forces of evil.

- Spiritual armor helps us in our struggle against evil.

- Praying in the Spirit is an effective and powerful method of praying.

Answers to Lesson 10

1. Deceives the whole world

2. Authority

3. Drive out evil spirits and heal every disease and sickness

4. Flee from you

5. The Lord

6. Rulers, authorities, powers of this dark world, spiritual forces of evil in the heavenly realms

7. Belt of truth

8. Breastplate of righteousness

9. As shoes for your feet, having put on the readiness given by the gospel of peace

10. The shield of faith

11. The helmet of salvation

12. The sword of the Spirit

13. Satan

14. Your answer

15. Praying in tongues; See 1 Corinthians 14:14-15.

16. Always

17. They understood Isaiah 53:4-5 as referring to physical ailments.

18. Call for the elders of the church to pray over the sick person, anointing the sick person with oil in the name of the Lord.

Our Prayer
For You

Our goal at *Global Initiative: Reaching Muslim Peoples* in producing this resource has been to bless you. Whether you are new in the Christian faith or have been following Jesus for many years, studying the timeless truths herein makes each of us *"wise for salvation"* (2 Timothy 3:15). Whether you find yourself in a community of believers or are in a season of solitude, we pray that you would sense the powerful and imminent presence of Jesus as you go forward in your faith in Him, the One who *"sets the lonely in families"* (Psalm 68:6, NIV). May He be the answer to all your questions, the satisfaction of your deepest longings, and be known as the One who carries you through your greatest difficulties. As Jesus told His disciples in John 16:33, *"In the world you will have tribulation. But take heart; I have overcome the world."* Jesus still overcomes today, and has made us overcomers in Him (Romans 8:37). Be persistent in your Christian faith today, knowing that,

God is able to keep you from stumbling and to present you blameless before the presence of his glory with great joy, to the only God, our Savior, through Jesus Christ our Lord, be glory, majesty, dominion, and authority, before all time and now and forever. Amen. (Jude 1:24-25)

APPENDIX

Lunar Calendar

Each Friday, Muslims all over the world join for Jumaa (Friday) prayers. On this Muslim day of community worship, adherents come together in the mosque at noon for prayers. Muslims follow a lunar calendar. The following chart identifies the months of the calendar and specific holidays.

Day	Title of Event	Comments
	Muharram	
1	*Ras al-Sana* The Muslim New Year	
10	*Ashura* A day of voluntary fasting	For Shi'ites, this day commemorates the death of Husayn, the son of Ali and grandson of Muhammad.
	Safar	

Rabi' I

12   *Maulid al-Nabi*

The Birthday of the Prophet

Some veneration of Muhammad takes place on this day; this holiday is widely observed, but discouraged in some places like Saudi Arabia.

Rabi' II

Jamadi I

Jamadi II

Rajab

27   *Lailat al-Isra wa al-Mi'raj*

Night of the Journey and the Ascension

This holiday is in remembrance of the night a winged animal took Muhammad from Mecca to the al-Aqsa mosque in Jerusalem and then up to heaven and back to Mecca on the same night. It is observed by prayers and recitation of the Quran.

Sha'ban

14   *Lailat al-Bara'a*

Night of Repentance

Commemorates a night when God descends to the lowest heaven to call to man and to grant forgiveness for sins. In some places, people say prayers for the dead, give food to the poor, and eat sweets. In some places, people treat it like a New Year's celebration.

Ramadan

27   *Lailat al-Qadr*

The Night of Power and Greatness

Commemorates the time when Muhammad received his first revelation; pious Muslims pray the entire evening in hopes that Allah will answer their prayers during this season of fasting.

Shawwal

1   *Id al-Fitr*

The Feast of Breaking the Fasting Month

This is a day of feasting. It is a celebratory time with lots of food and sweets and family visits.

Dhul-Qu'da

Dhul-Hijjah

1-10   The obligatory time of *hajj* for able-bodied Muslims once in their lifetime

Muslims must make a pilgrimage to the place they say Abraham offered to sacrifice Ishmael.

10   *Id al-Adha*

The Feast of Sacrifice

This holiday marks the end of the pilgrimage. They slaughter a sheep, cow, or camel, which commemorates the sacrificing of an animal in place of Ishmael. This is a festive time with family visits, gifts, and feasting

SUGGESTED READING AND WEBSITE RESOURCES

Abu, Da'ud. *Overview of Discipleship in Discipling Muslim Background Believers*. Self-published, 2019. Kindle.

Boa, Kenneth D. *Conformed to His Image: Biblical and Practical Approaches to Spiritual Formation*. Grand Rapids, MI: Zondervan, 2001.

Durie, Mark. *Liberty to the Captives: Freedom from Islam and Dhimmitude through the Cross*, 2nd ed. USA: Deror Books, 2013.

Frank, Audrey. *Covered Glory: The Face of Honor and Shame in the Muslim World*. Eugene, OR: Harvest House, 2019.

Geisler, Norman, and Abdul Saleeb. *Answering Islam: The Crescent in Light of the Cross*. Grand Rapids, MI: Baker Books, 2002.

Gilchrist, John. *Facing the Muslim Challenge: A Handbook of Christian - Muslim Apologetics*. 2nd ed. Cape Town, South Africa: Challenge Africa, 2002.

Gilchrist, John. *The Christian Witness to the Muslims.* Benoni, South Africa: Jesus to the Muslims, 1986.

Global Initiative: Reaching Muslim Peoples. *Journey to Understanding: Equipping Christians to Engage Muslims with Faith.* Springfield, MO: Onward Books, 2018.

Little, Don. *Effective Discipleship in Muslim Communities: Scripture, History and Seasoned Practices.* Downers Grove, IL: InterVarsity Press, 2015.

Loewen, Joy. *Woman to Woman: Sharing Jesus with Muslim Women.* Grand Rapids, MI: Chosen, a Division of Baker Publishing, 2010.

Malek, Sobhi. *Islamic Exodus into Freedom in Christ. 2008.*

Masood, Steven. *Into the Light: A Young Muslim's Search for Truth.* 2nd ed. United Kingdom: Paternoster 2002.

McCurry, Don. *Healing the Broken Family of Abraham: New Life for Muslims.* Ministries to Muslims, 2011.

Miller, Denzil R. *Power Encounter: Ministering in the Power and Anointing of the Holy Spirit,* 3rd ed. Springfield, MO: PneumaLife Publications, 2013.

Miller, Duane Alexander. *Living among the Breakage: Contextual Theology-Making and Ex-Muslim Christians.* Eugene, OR: Pickwick Publications, 2006.

Murray, Andrew. *The Essential Words of Andrew Murray: 12 Complete Books Covering the Entire Christian Life.* Uhrichsville, OH: Barbour Publishing, 2008.

Qureshi, Nabeel. *Seeking Allah, Finding Jesus: A Devout Muslim Encounters Christianity.* Grand Rapids, MI: Zondervan, 2014.

Reddin, Opal L. *Power Encounter: A Pentecostal Perspective.* Springfield, MO: Central Bible College Press, 1999.

Sheikh, Bilquis. *I Dared to Call Him Father: The Miraculous Story of a Muslim Woman's Encounter with God.* Grand Rapids, MI: Chosen Books, 2003.

Website Resources

Answering Islam: answering-islam.org

Answering Islam addresses many pertinent issues to Christians from a Muslim background, such as: Who is God? Who is Jesus? What is Christianity? It also provides testimonies of why Muslims came to faith in Jesus Christ. It is available in 27 languages.

Answering Muslims: answeringmuslims.com

Answering Muslims is a Christian apologetics website dedicated to responding to the questions, objections, and arguments of Muslims. The site is run by Christian debaters, lecturers, and writers who have a special interest in Islam.

Bible Brief: 2008biblebrief.com

BibleBrief provides a brief overview of the entire Bible. It includes maps, timelines, hyperlinks, charts, color-coded text, extensive biblical references, and slideshow presentations.

Evidence for God's Unchanging Word:
unchangingword.com

This website provides an online library of rational evidence for the reliability and validity of God's Word.

Global Initiative: Reaching Muslim Peoples:
reachingmuslimpeoples.com

Global Initiative is part of Assemblies of God World Missions and focuses on equipping the church to reach Muslims with the Good News of Jesus. The website provides resources to help believers acquire Jesus' heart for Muslim people and resources to equip them for evangelism to Muslim people.

Joshua Project: joshuaproject.net

This is an excellent resource for learning about what God is doing among the people groups of the world. They offer global prayer digests, podcasts, and helpful apps.

Jumaa Prayer: jumaaprayer.org

Join Jumaa Prayer, a global prayer movement that prays for the salvation of Muslims around the world. It provides specific prayer requests for each Friday of the year. An app is available for easy access.

JourneyOnline: journeyonline.org

This website provides hope for hurting people by addressing thirteen heartfelt issues commonly experienced by people worldwide, including, anxiety, depression, death, guilt, hopelessness, insignificance, and shame.

Mark Durie: Markdurie.com

This website provides thought-provoking articles that address current issues regarding monotheistic faiths, human rights, and religious freedom.

Muslims Ask: muslimsask.com

This website provides answers to common questions Muslims ask.

Network 211: network211.com

Network211 uses 21st century technology to communicate the 1st century gospel by helping people discover and grow in their journey with God.

Operation World: operationworld.org

Operation World provides a definitive resource for praying for all the nations of the world.

Prayer Cast: prayercast.com

This website focuses on activating world-changing prayer for the lost. They provide outstanding prayer videos related to issues pertinent to Christians from a Muslim Background.

Say Hello: sayhelloinfo.com

Say Hello is part of *Global Initiative: Reaching Muslim Peoples.* It provides resources to equip Christian women to "Say Hello" to Muslim women and begin a relationship with them. The resources help women overcome cultural and religious hindrances so they can effectively share the truth about Jesus with them.

For information regarding resources, visit the
Global Initiative: Reaching Muslim Peoples website

www.reachingmuslimpeoples.com

or

Say Hello website

www.sayhelloinfo.com

Other Resources Available

Intercede

The *Intercede* is a bi-monthly publication that provides in-depth articles
concerning Islam and lists prayer needs that relate to Muslim issues.
The resource is **free** in both online and hardcopy formats.
Sign up to receive the *Intercede* on the Global Initiative website.
Available in English, Spanish, and French

Book by Global Initiative

*Journey to Understanding: Equipping Christians to
Engage Muslims with Faith*

Available in Engish and Spanish; Cost: $5.00

Booklets

Questions Muslims Ask

Responding to Muslims

Sharing your Faith with Muslims

What Christians Need to Know About Muslims

Free as downloadable PDFs on the Global Initiative website.
Hardcopies are also available for purchase.
Available in English and Spanish